NATURAL HEARTLANDS

Previous Page: Sunset at the Giant's Causeway in County Antrim, Northern Ireland.

Opposite: St. Abb's Head, a National Trust for Scotland/Scottish Wildlife Trust nature reserve.

NATURAL HEARTLANDS

The landscape, people and wildlife of Britain and Ireland

David Woodfall and Kenneth Taylor

SWAN·HILL
PRESS

For Tesni, Ronan, Alice and Caroline with love.

Photographs Copyright © 1997 David Woodfall
Text Copyright © 1997 Dr Kenneth Taylor

First published in the UK in 1997
by Airlife Publishing Ltd

British Library Cataloguing-in-Publication Data
   A catalogue record for this book
   is available from the British Library

ISBN 1 85310 558 9

Typeset by Phoenix Typesetting, Ilkley, West Yorkshire.
Printed in Hong Kong

Airlife Publishing Ltd
101 Longden Road, Shrewsbury, SY3 9EB, England

Acknowledgements

David Woodfall would especially like to thank Brian and Sally Shuel and Peter Corkhill for help and support at critical times. Richard Moles for firing his imagination with ecology before it was a widely known term. Stephen Dalton for his enthusiasm for the idea of this book. Mark Edwards for help and advice in selecting the images. All the people who he has photographed and who often appeared when he had given up hope at the end of a long day. Laurie Whitehead of Swaledale and Robbie of Air Alba for a hair-raising flight over the Flow Country. His parents, Bill and Joyce, who have been supportive of all his wild enthusiasm. Marion Partington for much-appreciated special assistance. Martin Barlow and everyone at Woodfall Wild Images for all their hard work support.

Kenny Taylor would like to acknowledge an abiding debt of gratitude to his father, the late George Taylor, for sharing some of his storycraft, and to his mother, Doris Taylor, for instilling some of her boundless enthusiasm for history and learning. Caroline Vawdrey deserves special thanks for her support and for typing the manuscript.

Contents

A mute swan feeding on water crowfoot in the River Dee in North Wales.

THE HALCYON CONNECTION

Submerging slowly in the shallow river, I feel its coolness engulf me. The sounds of breeze and birdsong give way to a muffled drumming on the ears as water presses-in all around. The beat of the river's movement is all-embracing.

Seen through the glass of my snorkel mask, a yellow-green glow suffuses the water, where suspended particles glint in filtered sunlight as they tumble past. A school of minnows splashes to the side. The little fish seek shelter from my alien form by hiding near the stems of a bankside plant. I move cautiously towards this greenery until I can see their fixed stares and the silvering of their scales.

The decades since I last watched minnows closely – then with a few held captive in a jar – dissolve. But this is a very different encounter. For I can sense, for the first time, something of the wildness of these fish – savour the encounter for it being one where I am balanced precariously in their element, not they in mine. Above us, strands of floating vegetation stretch in a lattice against the brightness of the sky.

As one, the minnows flick away and merge with the shadows. Clutching the river bed, I move out from the bank. Beneath, the subtle patterns of gravel and mud unfold – here heaped in a tiny pile, there laid in rippling bands or smoothed and soft for a metre or so – a beauty in their variation. A caddis-fly larva, encased in a tube stuck with small pebbles, shuffles over this patterned surface, making for the edge of a large boulder, whose contours, in their turn, have been shaped by the river's flow.

Out in mid-stream, the current is strong, the sensation very different from the gentler, warmer shallows. Here, the force of water bubbling with oxygen is fit to challenge a trout as it pushes upstream to gain its spawning grounds. Clinging to rocks, I push my own body clear of the current and emerge, gasping and blinking, in bright sunlight, invigorated by the cleansing touch of pure water and by contact with the natural gradations of tone, texture and life in its channel.

Hauling-out to dry on an islet of shingle, the airborne sounds seem astonishingly varied – the movement of leaves on bankside willows, a sedge warbler reeling out a jazzy scramble of notes from the reeds, a redshank calling an alarm from a fence post by a riverside meadow, where lady's smock and buttercups stud the turf.

Not one of these species is scarce in Britain or Ireland. But their combination, blended with the noise of the river which sustains them and their living space, and whose channel is largely unaltered by human shaping, is now rare indeed. I savour the moment, washing my ears with its ebbs and flows of sound.

Rivers are prime movers and shapers of landscape, some as old as the rocks they cut through; a living presence with an ancient past. In England, for example, the beginnings of major river systems go back some seventy million years – to the twilight of the dinosaurs – when chalky sea waters shrank away and a land mass heaved up, rising faster in the west than in the east. The result was a generally eastward-sloping drainage pattern, with three dominant rivers – direct ancestors of the Dee and Trent, Thames, Frome and Solent. Although swamped again for a while by later inrushes of ocean, this basic drainage pattern remained broadly intact when the land was revealed once more.

In their time, these and other rivers have helped to move mountains of material from high ground to low, from land to sea, and have themselves been shunted by gargantuan forces in successive ice ages. Long after the last ice sheets vanished, the names that early inhabitants gave to the rivers which helped to transport, feed and water them, stuck.

River names are linguistic survivors. They comprise a high percentage of the names taken over by the Anglo-Saxons from the British tribes, according to philologist Margaret Gelling. These include some names which may be earlier still, perhaps learnt by early Celtic immigrants from Bronze Age inhabitants.

But if persistence is one feature of rivers and their names, change, movement and flux are other parts of the essential nature of river systems. There is infinite scope for variation of details, both small-scale and large, from the finer points of bank shape, to the broad course of channels. Whether over dizzying spans of geological time, the course of seasons, or in a single day – when heavy rains or snowmelt can work an awesome transformation – rivers are a latent force for change; a power disregarded at our peril.

Just once have I seen this process at work in an extreme way in Britain. A few years ago, I lived in the Highland hamlet of Laggan, in a cottage situated a few hundred metres away from the infant River Spey – a major water for many reasons, not least its importance for salmon fishing and for cooling the steams of the whisky distilleries along its length. In its track to the sea at the Moray Firth, the Spey includes both fast-flowing upland reaches, and broader, more easygoing lowland stretches. But it can be whisked to a frenzy in spate.

One night, I went to bed hearing not a whisper from the nearby water as it eased along its narrow channel through the Laggan flood-plain. Next morning, I awoke to an ominous rumbling beyond the house. Looking out of the dormer window, I saw, with a mixture of amazement and anxiety, that the river had been transformed beyond recognition.

Across half a kilometre of flood plain, fast-moving water, muddy with silt, flecked with spume and capped by waves, was speeding past. The gentle, infant watercourse had become a swollen demon of a torrent, engulfing the strath and threatening the very walls of the houses near its grasp. A few hours later, it subsided. But its main channel was reshaped, some trees and shingle bars had gone, and my perception and respect for one of the great elemental forces at work on the planet had changed utterly.

There is something inescapably organic about a river's changes, adding to the sense of it as a living presence in the landscape – as if it were a kind of super-being. This perception is further strengthened by considering a map of the network of waters, from smallest burns and feeders to major channels, which make up the entire catchment of a river from source to sea. From the core of the main river, interconnections branch outwards, and upwards. It is a cascade of linkages, whose pattern suggests a branching tree, or the blood vessels of a lung.

In general, a river's size is controlled by the area of its catchment, so that large rivers tend to have large catchments and so on. Slope, rainfall, vegetation cover and the type of rock underlying it, whether relatively porous, or resistant to downward seepage, also have a fundamental influence on a river's character.

British and Irish rivers are tiddlers in a global context, mostly fairly short and draining modest catchments. Of the 1,445 river systems in mainland Britain, for example, only twenty top 100 kilometres in length, and none drains a catchment larger than 10,000 square kilometres. The Thames, from its source at Trewsbury Mead near Cirencester to its sink beyond London, is the longest British river, although, as with all rivers which disgorge into wide estuaries, the seaward boundary can be a matter of some debate.

Ireland's longest river is the grand and softly curving Shannon. This languorous beauty of a water rises in the Leitrim plateau and wends its way through the great loughs of Allen, Ree, and Derg, before breasting the Atlantic swell beyond Limerick.

What most British and Irish rivers lack in length, they make up for in terms of sheer numbers and character. It is hard to go more than a few kilometres in these islands without being in easy reach of a river, which can be as redolent of regional variations as any more static feature of the landscape. The serpentine meanders of rivers winding through the flatlands of south-east England; the rivers which have fashioned their own steep gorges in the west; the braided channels of northern spate rivers; the weedy shallows of the waters in the Irish Midlands; and the clear chalk streams of the south of England, reflect, in their form, chemistry and character, some essential features of the countryside they both drain and replenish, erode and build.

Plants are a vital part of that regional distinctiveness. Thanks in large measure to work carried out by botanists such as Nigel Holmes, Sarah Haslam and John Rodwell, and developed as a working classification in the 1980s, there is now a clear picture of what types of river plant communities can be expected in any part of Britain. No Welsh or Scottish river has a 'chalk river' community, for example, and so usually lacks plants such as reed, blue water speedwell, brook water-crowfoot and great tussock sedge, which are abundant in many southern watercourses.

The plants of food-rich rivers of East Anglia also have little in common with the vegetation of nutrient-poor upland rivers, where the greenery often keeps a low profile on boulders and banksides. Mosses and liverworts are the characteristic dwellers of many upland waters. These flow fast in their steep descent to the coast and are a world apart from the slow-moving rivers of the lowlands, which can nurture a tall and leggy luxuriance along their gentle, silt-rich descent.

The plant life in a river supports many other kinds of life, from crustacea, insects and fish, to mammals and birds. Submerged and floating plants provide shelter for small fish, both from possible predators and from some of the rough rides of the current. They can be nibbled as food, give a platform for fish eggs and for some of the creatures which fish eat, or provide a jungle of possibilities for aquatic snails and beetles. The greenery which is rooted on the river bed, but thrusts clear of the water surface, can serve all of these functions and more besides, giving camouflage and anchorage to a moorhen's nest, a song perch for a sedge warbler, or a stairway to heaven for an emerging dragonfly, ready to make its radical move from aquatic larva to free-flying adult insect.

Beyond the banks, where kingfishers and sand martins might breed, a lowland river in its unfettered state seeps refreshment to the plants on its flood plain. It can give both water and nourishment to vegetation still fortunate enough to have links to its seasonal outpourings, and to the moist alluvium of the soils it has spread over the riverlands.

People have been reworking the margins of British and Irish rivers for centuries in an effort to control their fiercest flows, and so reduce flooding, or reclaim wetland ground for cultivation. But as with so many changes to the countryside, the scale and pace of these modifications accelerated from the late 1940s onwards.

Most rivers in Britain, and many in Ireland, have now been heavily modified by works

Opposite: The River Windrush and grazed water meadows at Burford in Oxfordshire.

Below: Volunteer conservation workers cleaning out the River Beal at Shaw, near Oldham.

Chemical pollution running into the River Mersey at Widnes.

for drainage or navigation. Until little more than a decade ago, much of this work was characterized by an engineering approach so obsessed with containing peak flows that it ignored the vital assets of more organically shaped, less straightjacketed rivers. Removal or severe cutting of riverside trees and bushes, straightening of banks and dredging of channels reduced all too many lowland streams and rivers to a state akin to huge urban gutters, devoid of greenery and brutalized by the prevailing channel vision of the time.

I can well remember my own revulsion at encountering Stalinist river regimes, when revisiting favourite stretches of waterway in southern England after the chalk-dredgers and chainsaws had done their worst. The sense of loss at seeing nothing but mud where moorhens had once nested, and hawthorns uprooted, reedy fringes dumped beyond the bank and backwaters obliterated, was acute. This was not only because the works were unsightly, but because they were, in a very real sense, an offence against nature, denying many of the qualities for which lowland rivers could be most valued – including their fundamental importance to their flood plain.

The flow in a natural river system swells and falls gradually, keeping the flood plain soils moist for much of the year and trickling food over the land to benefit plants and wildlife. Sever the river from its surrounds by 'canalization', and the flows both mount and drain more rapidly. A formerly quiet river (prone to occasional fevered flushes), can become downright flashy, eroding its own bed and banks more rapidly and rocketing quick-fire current down its gun-barrel channel. Ironically, such works – often done with an eye to flood prevention and land drainage – can provoke flood problems downstream.

For wildlife, those dark days of river 'management' imposed heavy losses, essentially because the different living spaces – from channel, to bankside, to flood plain – became uninhabitable for many plants and creatures which had previously found food, shelter and breeding room in the more natural systems. The enforced separation of rivers and flood plains caused massive destruction of neutral and wet grasslands and loss of many marshy and boggy places, where a wealth of plants had once grown, and wading birds thrived. Between 1930 and 1980, many thousands of kilometres of British and Irish rivers were widened, deepened and straightened.

The dawn of a new era, which at last brought conservationists and river engineers together to work on planning new schemes and to reverse past damage, came shortly afterwards. Environmental effects were considered together with the needs of flood defence. An accord was struck, leading, by the end of the decade, to a partnership between practitioners of these previously competing interests as a central tenet of the newly formed National Rivers Authority.

By the late 1990s, this teamwork has flourished, with a wealth of practical information now readily available. By helping to restore a sense of ecological balance, of going with rather than against the flow, this approach is at last also helping to replenish some of the diversity which was lost in the previous few decades.

One creature which is benefiting from the new regime is the feathered splendour of the brooks – the kingfisher – a tiny bird with a powerful presence, most likely to brighten a day along slow-flowing English waters, and many Irish rivers in every county. Often seen as a momentary blur speeding past, the electric-blue flash of a kingfisher's colours leaves an after-image which lingers long in mind. Seemingly out of proportion to the kingfisher's size and the brevity of the sighting, this is somehow rendered all the more potent by its being such an elusive beauty.

Excellent fuel to keep the blue flash alight can come from very small fish – especially bullheads and minnows. Both of these fare well in the clear, shallow waters of the chalk-lands of southern and eastern England. But the chalk streams are famed for a larger lure which they hold for much bigger fishers. The brown trout, which comes in a huge variety of forms and colours and has thousands of different stocks in British and Irish river systems, seems particularly at home in languid chalk streams, as does its principal human pursuer – the fly-fisher. For water issuing from springs at the base of chalk escarpments has many fine qualities, which can be a boon to fish and fishermen alike.

The porous rock releases its water store slowly, and at a fairly constant temperature, filtering and cleansing it before sending it on its seaward way. Flows can be reasonably constant (although springs which feed 'winterbournes' at higher levels of a valley typically fail in summer), giving a stable support medium for aquatic life, which is further helped by dissolved minerals which can be absorbed by plants.

Chalk stream water-crowfoot – the typical plant of these waters – is an ideal platform for molluscs and insects favoured by trout. It also screens small fry and provides additional oxygen to give extra bubble to the champagne-tinted streams. Views in the choicest reaches of these waters can be suffused with the very essence of the riverine bounty of luscious lowland England. Meadows snuggle up to willows which bend waterwards above bankside rushes, their reflections hazy on a gently rippled surface, where clouds of mayflies move like dancing wisps, and trout rise to nudge the surface, the concentric rings of their contact rippling like a kiss blown from water to air.

Opposite: Water crowfoot on the River Wye in Powys.

The dry bed of the River Kennet in Wiltshire, a situation largely caused by water abstraction for agriculture.

Such peace can come at a hefty price, with fishing beats on prime chalk streams an expensive luxury, savoured by the few, but dreamt of by many among the multi-million-strong throng of British and Irish anglers. Of all these trout-rich waters, it is the River Test in Hampshire which holds the most sought-after fishing, with one stretch of some 24 kilometres, beside Stockbridge, its rarest jewel.

This is the domain of the Houghton Club, which has kept access to the fabled banks in its ownership an exclusive preserve ever since its foundation in 1823. In the nineteenth century it was Frederick Halford and his friends in the Houghton Club who developed the modern approach to fly-fishing. That approach was then refined by local heroes such as William Lunn, the 'genius of the Test', first in a lineage of Lunns who held the club's waters in their charge for over a century from 1887 onwards.

For the two dozen members of the Houghton Club and their invited friends, to fish the Test with anything other than a dry fly would now be unthinkable. Foibles of the British establishment aside, there is no denying the skill demanded by that painstaking attention to style. Dry-fly fishing is the culmination of a progression of human thought focused on the capture of trout. This moved from ideas about the need for imitation of natural insect prey to lure a fish, to further mimicry in the form of copying an insect's motion, to

presenting the mimic to an individual fish, then making it move to attract the attention of that one object of desire.

It is a method which requires total concentration, coupled with quiet precision, for its success. The fisher sees a trout and deftly casts a line upstream from it, letting the fly lookalike with the steely sting in its tail land gently on the water and float near the nose of the target. If the fish lunges, the line must be jerked at precisely the right moment to hook the quarry. It is a fascinating blend of quiet strategem and rapid action, whose prime British arena is set among the soft beauty of the chalk streams. Small wonder that it can cost a king's ransom to fish there.

But the riparian idyll of many chalk streams has not been immune from modern pressures, especially from shifts in land and water use beyond their banks. Heavy abstraction of water from boreholes in downland and elsewhere has sucked some springs in the valleys dry. Coupled with periods of prolonged drought, this has drastically reduced the flow of dozens of rivers. In the worst cases, such as has happened with the Ver in Hertfordshire, Misbourne in Buckinghamshire and the Darent in Kent, long stretches of the main river have dried up completely.

Additional impacts have come with increased pollution from nitrates and phosphates running down farm drains into the rivers, and from the conversion of most of the former channelside water-meadows to arable. The traditional chalk-stream scene, rich in wildlife variety, and with the ebbs and swells of its water dictated more by the seasons and rains than by humans and drains, is rarer now than ever before.

Worried by such changes, groups such as the Anglers' Co-operative Association have taken successful legal action to block plans to extract more water from small feeders which fill chalk streams in several counties. Community organizations have also formed in places such as the upper Thames valley, to argue more effectively for the restoration of healthier river flows and better water quality.

This widespread concern has begun to spread at a time when the National Rivers Authority has been making a major push to produce river 'management' plans of a very different kind from the plans of campaign used in the rash assaults of earlier decades. These take account of activities within entire catchments which could have a bearing on the rivers they feed. It is a logical step forward, attempting to restore natural linkages which have been lost. But it is also a daunting and difficult task, since it is hard to gather all the information, or influence all the people whose actions could affect a river's health.

Yet without such attempts, the future of some distinctive riverine wildlife could still hang in the balance. Most rivers have survived the severings and sourings of the last few decades – but some only just. The blue ribbons still snake through the lowlands, and the challenge now is to green them again. It should be well worth taking the plunge.

Opposite: A classic chalk stream — the River Itchen in Hampshire.

CALEDON REGAINED

In the slanting sunlight of early morning, mist swathes the old wood. Backlit, the vapour throws the shape and texture of trees and bushes into sharp relief. Whiteness shifts along stems and branches and distance is obliterated. Earth, trees and air seem filled with a primal breath.

Closer to, some colours are revealed. The bottle green of the old scots pines is prominent, their bark glowing deep red-brown in the strengthening day. Each one is an individual, with great arms twisting out in different patterns and directions. Some branches bear sprays of needles and cones, others are bare and skeletal. In places, an entire trunk stands hollow and crumbling, a great monument to a life which was rooted here for centuries.

Pale-stemmed birches crowd some of the spaces between the pines, their leaves a stippling of brighter, lighter green. In a few weeks from now, these birches will add cascades of gold to the scene – brilliant showers poised before final leaf fall. Here and there, a rowan tree pokes through, its clusters of berries already reddening for the autumn to come; or an aspen, grey-stemmed and elegant, shimmers its greenery in the slightest hint of breeze. Junipers, some tall, others low and bushy, add deep green froth to the middle levels, the lowest of their branches touching heather, grasses and small berry-bearing shrubs which sprout from the woodland floor. No sound breaks the stillness.

Time was, a brown bear could walk through trees such as these for hour after hour. Picture the journey: it starts at sunrise on a long summer's morning, and by midday the trees are still all around. The colour of foliage and stems of different species varies. In some places, where fire or wind-throw has punched a hole in the canopy, heather and blaeberry are thick underfoot, and small seedlings jostle for a place in the sun above the ground cover.

In others, forest bogs, squelching with saturated moss and fringed by alders at their margins, make progress difficult. Perhaps beavers have helped to keep the water levels high in these wetlands, where ospreys come to fish for trout and families of wild boar slake their thirst. Skirting a bog, the bear is back amongst trees; pines and birches are the commonest, but they mix in places with a surprising variety of others, such as hazels, willows, cherries and aspens. A thicket of young pines, close-packed and near impenetrable, bars the way, but to the side the going is easier, past widely spaced older pines. Deep claw marks in a trunk show that another bear passed by here not long before.

Through afternoon and evening – with more clearings, more thickets, more bogs and more variety – the trees are still abundant. By full darkness – which in this northern place comes twenty hours beyond daybreak – there is still no sign of reaching the forest's edge. Settling down to sleep for a while on a bed of springy heather, the calls of a wolf pack trouble the bear's slumber through the brief summer night.

That was then, before the return of people to Britain and Ireland after ice melt, when a true forest – some call it the 'Great Wood of Caledon' – cloaked much of the Scottish Highlands. Now, after millennia of destruction and change – brought about by shifts in climate, by human action through felling, burning and clearing, and by grazing from domestic stock and deer – most of the former cover of this, the greatest forest ever to grace our uplands, has gone. But it is no mere whimsy to hark back to its heyday. For the past – even the distant past – may give pointers to the future, when pines and other natives from the former upland woods, both in Scotland and elsewhere, could play a pivotal role in shaping new forests.

The scots pine is the only pine ever to have occurred naturally in Britain and Ireland. It is also the most widespread conifer in the world, so linking its name to the extreme western outpost of its range seems a splendid piece of island-dweller's cheek. On the continent, it grows in Iberia, and in a huge swathe of country from central Europe and Scandinavia, across Eurasia to the Pacific.

For the last two-and-a-half-million years, the fortunes of scots pines in Europe have waxed and waned with retreats and advances of successive ice sheets, in some twenty-three alternating colder and warmer periods. After the end of the last glaciation (as would have happened in other thaws, after other ice retreats), the gradual greening of the ice-scrubbed ground happened in slow motion waves of colonisation, as first one community of plants, then another, took over the land which had emerged afresh from the freeze.

Tundra, where reindeer herds grazed and lemmings nibbled and tunnelled through lichens and mosses, gave way to a scrub of juniper bushes, dwarf and downy birches, and aspens. Then the pines advanced, but from more than one direction. After spreading northwest across central Europe, they reached southern Britain more than 10,500 years ago, while the country was still linked by a land bridge to the continent. Mixed woods of pine, birch and hazel became abundant in southern England at that time; and a little later, hazel and pine followed on from willows and birches in Ireland.

But the southern advance was overtaken. Oak trees arrived and spread north and westwards, replacing pines as the dominant trees. Pedunculate oaks, bearing stalked acorns, gained lowland ground on richer soils, where they are still prevalent in the native woodland scene today, especially in the English Midlands. Sessile oaks, whose unstalked acorns sit close to their stems, took a grip in Ireland and in the western uplands, from Cornwall,

Opposite: Caledonian Forest with scots pine, sessile oaks and birches in the Glen Strathfarrar National Nature Reserve, Inverness-shire.

through Wales and northern England to the wooded glens of Highland Scotland's Atlantic fringe, where, mixed with birch, they still hold sway. When alders moved in, they shoved the scots pines out from lakesides, flood plains and other wetland margins. Within three thousand years of their southern arrival after the ice melt, the pine battalions beyond Scotland had retreated to higher ground and poorer soils.

But things were different in the country that would give the pines their modern name. Around 9,000 years ago, scots pines appeared in force in north-west Scotland. The parents of the seedlings in the vanguard of this settlement, in places like Wester Ross, were not the southern colonisers, but probably lived in a refuge to the south-west which had remained free of ice during the last cold period. Even today, pines in the western Highlands, such as in the Beinn Eighe National Nature Reserve, are a quite distinct race from those in the eastern Highlands, whose ancestral stock may have been Scandinavian.

Once rooted in Scotland, the pines went on a 4,500-year spree. Advancing on broad fronts, which moved forward at a few hundred metres each year, they spread up mountains to live at the limits of exposure that their leaves and seeds could tolerate. They pushed across lowlands and consolidated their position in the north-west, and in Strathspey and Deeside, the Galloway Hills and Rannoch Moor. At the peak of these balmy times, when the climate was warmer on average than it has been since (although that distinction seems to be rapidly vanishing), woodlands of all kinds flourished throughout Britain, and caledonian forests of pine and birch dominated the Scottish Highland scene.

Even when other woodlands began to decline – from some five thousand seven hundred years ago onwards, at a time when the climate was getting wetter, and the first farmers had arrived from the continent to make their mark – scots pines continued to expand. But their reprieve was short lived.

The rains helped blanket bogs to swell and smother former forest ground, while pressure from the new agriculturalists finally began to bite. The decline of the native upland trees continued for millennia after that.

By 1750, perhaps only about 5 per cent of the land surface of Scotland was wooded, compared with more than ten times that amount when the neolithic farmers arrived with their livestock. Pressure from increasing numbers of people, from grazing by cattle, then by goats, sheep and deer, from fires and war-time fellings and underplanting with introduced conifers, continued to take a toll in the two centuries that followed.

Yet all was not gloom, even in these later years, for people in some places had a strong vested interest in ensuring the continuity of woodland on their home ground. Although much reduced from their former extent, the pine and birch woods in caledonian forest strongholds, such as the straths and hillslopes beside the rivers Spey and Dee, played an important part in the local economy of these areas in the eighteenth and nineteenth centuries.

In Strathspey, Elizabeth Grant of Rothiemurchus – part of a dynasty which has owned one of the finest surviving pinewoods for generations – recorded in her memoirs for the year 1813 that 'the number of people employed in the forest was great'.

She describes, in lively detail, how pines were felled and dragged by horses to strategic positions in the forest. What followed was high drama, when heavy sluice gates, which had held water in artificially created ponds, were opened before daybreak to let-loose a torrent. Gangs of workmen were ready for the rush of water when it reached the log piles. Some rolled, some shoved, others leapt along the banks, prodding the timber to keep it moving towards the main river, where the 'Spey floaters' took over to shepherd the logs to sawmills further downstream.

Across the Cairngorms from Strathspey, in what was later to become known as 'Royal' Deeside, through the Windsor's link with Balmoral, far-sighted lairds had been taking steps to ensure the survival of productive native woodland on their ground since at least the early 1600s. Paramount among these pioneer tree planters was James Farqhuarson of Invercauld. He died in 1805, but by 1790 had been credited with planting 14 million pines (of local seed stock) and one million larch trees.

If some of the pine-dominated woods played a central role in local economies in past centuries, the upland oakwoods figured even more strongly in people's lives. Today, these woods are seen more as places where natural attractions are obvious and where human associations, except for the ubiquitous presence and impact of sheep flocks, are harder to discern.

There is no doubting the allure of these characterful upland oaks and their associated wildlife. Whether in a Devon combe, Welsh hillside, or beside a West Highland loch, they have a special atmosphere, produced, in part, from a combination of their lush and soft green set against starker rock, or steeply angled slopes and gorges. Each tree holds layer upon layer of colour and pattern.

The masses of leaves are translucent at first opening, becoming darker later as they thicken. Twigs, branches and trunks twist and curve, some bearing ferns aloft, most covered in thick growths of moss and lichen. The trees seem to drip with other vegetation, for in the moist coolness of Britain's western fringe their presence has allowed a kind of temperate rainforest to evolve.

This luxuriance comes, not so much from higher plants – bonny though the wood sorrel, primroses, violets and cow-wheat may be when they add their pastel freshness to the oakwood floors – but from small plants which lack sturdy veins to transport water through their structures. Most of these mosses and liverworts – or 'bryophytes' as botanists refer to them in tandem – are modest in size, but big on beauty and variety.

Britain and Ireland are spectacularly rich in bryophytes, holding more than two-thirds of the species recorded in Europe (in contrast to less than one-fifth of the higher plant species). The oceanic, or 'Atlantic', bryophytes of the western native oakwoods are particularly varied, making these places, by that token, the moss and liverwort treasure house of

Opposite: Horner Woods in the Exmoor National Park, Somerset, in an autumn rainstorm.

the continent. Even a modest-sized western oakwood can harbour 150 different kinds of them – a figure which would be impressive even in a tropical rainforest.

Hummocks of mosses can be common in many western oakwoods, and are prominent in some of the few remaining Irish fragments, but these are usually formed by large, unpalatable species. Rather than indicating healthy diversity, the tussocks often point to the widespread problem of overgrazing by sheep and deer.

Here, as in the upland pine- and birch-dominated woods, excessive nibbling is wearing the old oakwoods threadbare, destroying seedlings before they can grow to saplings, shifting the balance of plant life, rubbing surfaces clean of clinging vegetation and pushing the woods up and over the edge of oblivion. It is a far cry from the situation in earlier centuries, when the western oakwoods were highly valued as a source of renewable materials, and their medium-term future was secured by human intervention.

The history of upland woods has been only patchily documented, in contrast to the very detailed research on lowland native woods carried out in recent decades. But it is still apparent that many upland woods were exploited for coppice products – such as poles of different sizes sprouted from cut stumps of broadleaved trees – and used as woodland pastures for grazing and sheltering sheep and cattle.

Woodland management at a Coed Cymru project in Denbighshire.

For the western oakwoods, it was the onset of the Industrial Revolution which promoted their most intensive period of human use. Demand for tanbark and ship timber, and for charcoal to fuel the furnaces from whose white heat the iron in the soul of the revolution was being forged, added new value to timber products. The woods of Cumbria in north-west England were an early source of charcoal, but the Cumbrian ironmasters soon turned their gaze north of the border, where the oakwoods of Highland Scotland's Atlantic fringe offered a huge resource of excellent wood for charcoaling.

Unlike the sorry situation in Ireland at this time, the boom in north British charcoal production was no slash-and-burn rampage through surviving native woodlands. Rather, it seems to have been a carefully controlled business enterprise, which could involve long-term commitments to the purchase of wood from particular areas. When Robert Ford and Company – a Cumbrian firm which was later to become the biggest iron-making concern in north-west England - built their famous blast furnace at Bonawe near Oban in 1753, for example, it negotiated timbering contracts with a neighbouring clan chief for the next 110 years (not far short of the period during which the furnace actually operated).

Scotland's Historiographer Royal, Christopher Smout, has dubbed the 50 years from 1780 onwards as, in many respects, the country's 'golden age' of sustainable forestry, when oakwoods were intensively tended to boost their health and yield. Competing, less economically valuable trees, such as birch, holly and rowan were removed and woods were coppiced in a prudent rotation, often of about twenty years. New oakwoods were created by planting, and long-established ones were protected by fencing to exclude livestock.

The downside of this spirit of fresh enterprise was that its emphasis on the exclusion of grazing animals divorced farmers and neighbouring communities from care and contact with the woods. So when the market for tanbark and charcoal slumped after 1830, a tradition of local woodmanship – which could have spared many woodlands from the worst excesses of what was to come in the following century – had already gone.

The western oakwoods, rapidly shifted from community resource to big moneyspinners for a landowning minority in the eighteenth and early nineteenth centuries, were suddenly toppled to the status of no-nibbles-barred wood pastures, used year-round with scant regard for the health of the trees. A similar attitude began to prevail in other upland woods. The stage was set, both physically and in terms of people's attitudes, for much more radical changes which came in the wake of the foundation of the Forestry Commission in 1919.

Modern plantations – stands of timber grown to be completely felled over a few decades, rather than partially cropped and maintained over centuries – now dominate the woodland scene in the British uplands. Nearly half the total British area of commercially managed woodland lies north of Hadrian's Wall. Most of it comprises introduced species of conifers. One – the Sitka spruce – first brought to Britain in the 1830s by Scottish botanist and explorer David Douglas, is paramount, while others such as lodgepole pine, Douglas fir, larch and Norway spruce are widespread.

Particularly in the last 50 years, the expansion of new conifer plantations has completely altered the balance of tree cover in Scotland, Wales and northern England and has transformed whole landscapes. In Scotland as a whole, for example, the area of woodland has grown by more than three-quarters since the late 1940s, almost entirely due to conifer planting. Uplands – where land was cheapest during the peak twentieth-century push for increased production of home-grown timber – have borne the brunt of this change. But in some parts of the country, the conifers stretch from valley to hilltop, covering sweet ground and sour.

In the course of this transformation, many old woods were destroyed, either by the quick

Opposite:Conifer plantations around an area of dead scots pines in the Scottish Highlands.

dispatch of their native trees by felling or ringbarking, or by the slower death of under-planting. By this method, the established broadleaves and native conifers could give shelter as 'nurses' to the young exotics before the fast-growing implants overtopped and smothered them – cutting off light and depriving them of water.

Coupled with this death by strangulation was the bite of multi-millions of jaws, as burgeoning sheep flocks enjoyed free rein on the surviving stands of upland natives, and an ever-expanding stock of red deer added extra insult to multiple injury. The sight of grey and skeletal pines, surrounded by hectares of sitka; of ancient oakwoods and birchwoods collapsing with no young trees to replace them; and of caledonian forest fragments over billiard-table-level heaths, where excessive deer numbers had stopped tree regeneration for centuries, became an all-too-familiar upland scene in the late twentieth century.

But then, beginning just a few years ago, many different people began to work to pull the native uplanders back from the brink. Groups such as Re-Foresting Scotland began to campaign, vigorously and effectively, to draw attention to the plight of the old woods and the scope for change. Others, such Coed Cymru and Scottish Native Woods, began to involve communities, including children, in the care, planting and expansion of native trees. They, and others, such as Highland Birchwoods and green woodworking associations, started to explore economic uses for native timber and helped to blow the dust off techniques of woodmanship which had been shelved for generations. Trees for Life, while tackling practical forest restoration projects, drew attention to spiritual and inspirational aspects of living and working with trees.

Agencies too, sometimes goaded by this popular groundswell, began to rally to the cause. Detailed surveys by national bodies mapped out the general picture of decline and highlighted potential hotspots for promoting change. And the Forestry Commission – previously responsible for the destruction of many native upland stands - took to native greening with gusto, commissioning surveys, designating caledonian forest nature reserves and working in partnership with other groups – both statutory and voluntary, to put the old woods back in better heart. All this, combined with a new enthusiasm for researching and documenting the history of old woods, prepared the way for massive initiatives, such as the Millennium Forest for Scotland, which is now funding a wealth of different projects which aim to expand, cherish and celebrate native woods in both upland and lowland areas throughout Scotland.

For the Caledonian Forest at least, prospects are now brighter than they have been for at least two centuries. For the oakwoods of the west, there is still a tension, all too often, between sheep culture (operated in ways which threaten trees and reduce the variety of life within them) and woodland culture, which could help to focus on the needs of both trees and livestock. This is understandable, given the many livelihoods in upland areas which depend on a system of subsidy geared to quantity of animals, rather than quality of both the livestock and the environment which supports them.

Logically, a shift to a more benign and ecologically sound means of social and agricul-tural support in the uplands should be inevitable. Politically, of course, that need not necessarily be the case. But the energy of the upland tree-promoters suggests that it could yet move governments, if it succeeds in moving enough hearts and minds. For this is now one of the liveliest, most spirited, most successful and most rapidly expanding facets of British conservation effort in the late 1990s, embracing many kinds of partners, involving many different disciplines and with burgeoning strands of artistic, craftwork, and community-linked ventures.

Here at least, some natural links that were severed generations ago are now being restored. And in the process, it is not just Caledon that has been regained.

Opposite: An oakwood, carpeted with bluebells in the Snowdonia National Park, North Wales.

Below: A spectacular waterfall at Tomies Wood, in the Killarney National Park, Eire.

THE GREENERY OF DOMESDAY

The leaves of the lime trees catch the early morning light. Their translucent shapes seem to blink and shimmer, delicate as drying insect wings, bright as breeze-blown bunting against the woodland shade.

The flickering movement has an elusive beauty, and a strange poignancy. For these are small-leaved limes – some of the last survivors of a tree tribe that once held great swathes of the English lowlands, and more besides, in its fresh green sway. Now they cling on in abundance in precious few places, victims of changing climate, social trends and market forces.

For a few millennia after ice melt and tundra retreat, when summers were dry and hot, the small-leaved limes set seed, multiplied and thrived. Come the colder, wetter climate at the end of those balmy times, their fortunes changed. Through more than six thousand years, the warmth loving small-leaved lime has had a long, slow fade. But in the last hundred years or so, this has merged with a further retreat – the waning of trades, crafts and skills through which people made use of the old woods, both of lime and many other kinds of native broad-leaved trees, and with that use, valued and sustained them.

Each lime in this Lincolnshire woodland bears the unmistakable mark of human shaping. Several stems sprout from each tree bole, thrusting arms of timber upwards to hold the main mass of leaves aloft. Their thickness suggests that it is many years since woodmen last coppiced these trees, close-cropping the stems at their bases and leaving the cut stumps to sprout afresh.

Before that final cut, perhaps every fifteen years or so, these people, and many generations of their forebears, would have done something similar. Fifty such coups could have punctuated the divide between this wood's first use as a coppice, back in the Middle Ages when monks tended the trees here, and the visit of the last woodmen. But a single tree could span that gap.

Knowledge of continuity across great lengths of time can add an important dimension to perception of a place, especially when you walk, not simply on its surface, but within its very structure. Surrounded by stems which push upwards for several metres then arch overhead, and musing about monks and woodmen, I feel enveloped by a sense of shifting time – of the past within the dappled light and forms of the present – a sensation akin to walking among the pillars of a medieval church.

The wood's real significance begins to press home. Cultural links, attractiveness of shapes and patterns, and richness of wildlife are all part of it; (I know where wild lily of the valley spreads nodding blooms across half an acre under this wood, where woodcocks squeak above clearings at dusk, and where butterflies vie to win sunspot territories). But there is something more – a response that defies easy pigeon-holing within rational categories.

I step up and over an old earthwork bank and walk clear of the wood, looking out at the yellow glare of oilseed rapé fields and the flatness of a prairie landscape, jolted into a precise and unmistakable present. Yet something of what I have just left still tugs and teases.

The grove is more than just trees, I think; it is a place where you can sense the slow rhythms of another beat of life. I walk away, with a pagan pulse drumming in my ears.

Particular details of the small-leaved lime's slide from surfeit to dearth are a special case within the history of Britain and Ireland's native lowland woodlands. But the general themes – of reduction from the luxuriance of the distant past, then long and largely positive association with people, then dissociation and loss – hold much more widely true. Each country has its variations.

In Ireland, (where the original woodland cover was strong on elm and hazel) really large expanses of forest had gone by some 1700 years ago, although extensive stands of hazel and woods of sessile oak were still widespread. The richness of that green cloak is still almost palpable, across a thousand years, in the words of an anonymous Irish writer of the tenth century, describing the scene near his woodland hut:

> A tree of apples of great bounty . . . huge; a seemly crop from small-nutted branching green hazels, in clusters like a fist . . . The songs of the bright-breasted ring doves, a beloved movement, the carol of the thrush, pleasant and familiar above my house. Swarms of bees, beetles, soft music of the world, a gentle humming.

By the sixteenth century, people with power to influence the broad-scale look of the land had begun to see the surviving Irish woods as more of a bane than a blessing – a refuge for rebels and the haunt of wolves. Tudor conquests paved the way for colonisation by new settlers and ushered in several centuries of woodland destruction, buoyed-up by a rise in demand for oak bark for tanning, charcoal for iron smelting and planks for barrels, house frames and ships.

Coppicing had been a strong tradition in Celtic and Viking Ireland, but it had generally declined by the seventeenth century. So the exploitation of woods for such products, rather than being a cropping to exploit a sustainable resource, seems often to have entailed their destruction.

Opposite: A sow and her piglets grazing in the New Forest in Hampshire during the pannage season. The pigs eat the abundant acorns which are poisonous to the forest ponies.

The Green Man in Norwich Cathedral in Norfolk.

Pressure on the Irish woods grew further with the massive growth of the Irish population, which peaked at over eight million by the 1840s (twice the present level), before plummeting through the ravages of the Great Famine and mass emigration. Trees had covered perhaps one-eighth of Ireland's land surface in Tudor times, but by 1800 this wooded portion had shrunk to one-fiftieth, and by the early years of this century, to one two-hundredth.

The 'soft music' of the native woods was all but gone. It was confined to fragments beyond the reach of agricultural reclamation, or protected within the bounds of large country estates. Ireland had become the least wooded country in Europe – a dubious distinction which it still holds today, even after many decades of planting of exotic conifers in commercial stands.

Sessile oak, whose Gaelic name is still sprinkled like an almost forgotten benediction over the map of Ireland in the many 'derry' places once named in its honour, now remains abundant only in a few deep valleys, especially in parts of Wicklow, Connemara and Donegal, and in the estate woodlands of the Killarney National Park. Heavily grazed by sika deer and sheep, the Killarney oakwoods have a strange beauty which borders on the eerie for anyone more used to the multi-layered vibrancy of oakwoods in Britain. Masses of oak branches, thick with lichens and sprouting with ferns, corkscrew out from trunks whose roots clasp ground where few herbaceous plants can grow. Mosses, liverworts and filmy ferns smooth every boulder and tussock, cloaking the floor in a sound-deadening mantle.

Goldcrests cheep in the canopy, but there are none of the birds which can give a distinctive oaky tang to a woodland chorus east of the Irish Sea. For pied flycatchers, wood warblers, redstarts and tree pipits are almost unknown in these or any other Irish woods, and woodpeckers of any kind are totally absent.

This lack of bird variety – a legacy of Ireland's distance from the main continental mass of Europe and of the flooding of the sea divide between it and Britain – is balanced, to some extent, by surprises in other fauna, such as the fairly widespread red squirrels, and an elusive but thriving pine marten population. But the old Irish woods still sit somewhat uneasily in their few remaining havens, native strangers not yet fully welcomed in the land beyond their narrow bounds.

In Scotland, the story has different emphases, although some of the strands are similar. Now, native woodlands cover only one-hundredth of Scotland. Their principal refuge is in the Highlands, where woodlands dominated by scots pine and birch trees comprise a staggering ninety percent of the country's surviving expanse of native trees. These northern woods of the Scottish uplands are western outliers of the boreal forests, with stronger links to the conifer-dominated systems of Scandinavia and beyond than to the broadleaved woods on the softer side of the Highland Line.

Through the rest of Britain and all of Ireland, the woodland ties are to the broadleaved woods of north-west Europe's Atlantic fringe. Along coasts and across islands, from Portugal to central Norway, trees such as oaks, ash, hazel, beech and birches set the keynote, with others such as elm, maple, hornbeam and willows, and shrubs such as bramble, hawthorn and honeysuckle, as the leitmotif.

In England and Wales, as in Scotland, some of the changes which massively reduced the original forest expanses happened a very long time ago. Before the arrival of Neolithic farmers, small-leaved lime was still the commonest tree in the English lowlands. But there was variety in and beyond its realm, with substantial tongues of ashwoods along scarps and other chalky soiled places in the south and east; pedunculate oaks establishing themselves in rich lowland ground; great tracts of alderwood in the tidal flatlands of major estuaries; birches and sessile oaks in the northern uplands; and much other local variation besides.

To the west, the sessile oak was the most widespread tree in Devon and Cornwall, across most of Wales and in Cumbria. There was also a substantial swathe of hazel- and elm-rich woodland in south-west Wales (an echo of Ireland's predominant tree cover at that time). With the arrival of the farmers, things began to change rapidly as ground was cleared to make way for crops and grazing animals.

It is possible that half of England had ceased to be wooded by the early Iron Age, with further reductions in Roman times. In typical midland counties of what Oliver Rackham, foremost chronicler of British ancient woodlands, terms 'planned countryside' (a land long characterized by extensive farms, sparse hedges, few heaths and little woodland) most of the great native woods had vanished centuries before the Domesday Book was compiled in 1086.

In the 'ancient countryside' counties (typified by thick hedges and hedgerow trees, winding lanes and holloways, small farms, many woods and scattered heaths), the Romans left much woodland intact, so that the land here was more than twice as wooded in 1086 as that in the future 'planned countryside'. Despite major inroads through woodland clearance in the two-and-a-half centuries of population boom before the Black Death, and many changes in recent decades, this distinction has remained.

Wales may have been rather more wooded than England and lowland Scotland at the time of the Domesday Book, but many of its woods suffered a gradual decline in the centuries which followed, both by felling and by increasing grazing pressure from livestock. Excessive nibbling by sheep is still the bane of many Welsh woods, as it is, through grazing by both sheep and red deer, in the Scottish uplands.

But, as also happened in both Scotland and northern England, a great surge of interest in the production of timber to provide some of the stuff which powered the industrial revolution helped – perhaps surprisingly – to protect many Welsh woods which might otherwise have been felled in the eighteenth and nineteenth centuries. Oakwoods, which yielded charcoal for iron smelting, bark for tanneries and, later, timber for coal shafts, were mostly cared for as a lucrative, sustainable asset. Only in the late nineteenth and early twentieth centuries, when the market for such products had waned or been changed by imports of foreign-produced material, did the surviving ancient woods of the Rhondda, Ebbw Vale and other valleys – until that time among the most wooded parts of Britain – begin to topple to the axe, or suffer slow attrition by being left open for sheep.

The First World War was a further great woodland leveller, both in Wales and in much of the rest of Britain, when many tracts of native woods were felled to provide pit props for the coalfields and other timber for the war effort. The establishment of the Forestry Commission in 1919, following the end of that conflict, was a major turning point for the future of Britain's native trees.

During most of the rest of the century, those natives were relegated to the status of sylvan underclass by government policies, implemented by the Forestry Commission, which sought to boost the national reserve of timber primarily through widespread planting of fast-growing conifers. The rise of plantation forestry, especially in vast stands of sitka spruce and other exotic conifers, worked major transformations in many landscapes. This was, and still is, especially the case in the uplands (see 'Caledon Regained'). But it also took a huge toll on native trees, even in choice lowland places such as the New Forest.

And there were other powerful forces which had already been pushing against the native woods, long before the advent of state-backed conifer forestry. From the nineteenth century onwards, loss of markets for woodland products put the squeeze on the old ways of woodmanship. Goods of plastic, metal and imported timber became cheaper or more convenient than those from the native trees, and coal distributed on the new railway

Right: A dead oak tree looms through mist in Sherwood Forest.

network meant that fuel wood could be neglected. Whether on hearth-fire or table, sheep-fold or washing line, the rout of the wood goods was crushing.

With the loss of such links to the remaining woods – previously cherished as providers of renewable energy, food and other materials – the way had been prepared for the onslaught which followed. By the middle of this century, there were precious few people left who could remember the worth of the old woodland skills. It would then have seemed logical, as well as profitable, for farmers to view the disused woods as land ripe for ploughing, or for state foresters to think of transforming them, in their speak, to 'produc-tive' woodlands in the form of new plantations.

In England and Wales, the most recent losses of ancient tree cover were particularly speeded by a demand for expansion of farmland after the 1940s. The toll in some counties was heavy indeed. In Gwynedd, for example, some two-thirds of the ancient woodland which had survived until the 1940s had gone by the mid-1980s. In Northamptonshire and Shropshire, the loss was similar. In other counties, reductions of one-third to a half were the average.

In less than the working lifetime of one forester, numerous woodlands which had figured in the lives of many generations, some from Anglo-Saxon times or earlier, were obliterated. Their demise was a bitter one, for these places represented some of the last shreds of connection to the natural tree cover which had burgeoned many thousands of years earlier, and which had been the living framework for a long history of intimate human use, which, in its turn, had helped to mould the very structure of such places.

Paramount among the methods used to shape and crop woodlands to serve human ends in the past was coppicing. In this, trees were cut at intervals, usually of between five and

Lowland wood being destroyed for development, North Wales.

twenty years, then allowed to regrow from their stumps or 'stools'. By dividing a wood into compartments, only some of which were cut in any one year, the copse could be worked on a rotation, providing a steady crop of coppice poles from its underwood. Standard trees, scattered among the stools but allowed to grow tall, could yield larger timbers for use in house or ship construction. Husbanded in this way, a woodland of only a few hectares could provide the entire timber needs of a woodman, such as someone who split and wove hazel stems to make hurdles for livestock, throughout a whole working career.

The bonus of such rolling coppice programmes for wildlife is that, within an actively worked wood, they maintain a patchwork of areas from open ground through the early, bushy stages of succession to high forest. This particularly suits a range of plants and crea-tures which thrive in bright conditions or at the margins of clearings, and can give some of the most striking effects of colour and sound to the woodland scene from a human perspective.

Low-growing, spring flowering plants are part of the bunch which benefits. Primroses, oxlips, celandines and wood anemones early in the season, bluebells, red campions and orchids later – the classic floral colourists of the vernal lowland woods – can all be boosted by the flood of light which bathes their seedbeds after coppice stems are felled.

Once stools sprout more densely, with brambles scrambling round, summer-visiting songsters such as whitethroats, blackcaps and garden warblers home in, using the low and leafy cover for nesting, and the taller stems or standard trees for shouting territorial claims. Prime time for nightingales in southern coppice woods is a short while later. They usually add their luscious outpourings to particular parts of the woods for only a few years before moving on as stems grow tall and the shrubbery thins.

Many insects can gain too, including butterflies, such as the several kinds of fritillary which use violets as food plants for their caterpillars and other blossoms as nectar sources to fuel them through the summer days. Colour, song, fluttering wings and new greenery – a beguiling blend, but only part of the full woodland picture.

For the losers in a coppice regime can be the life forms which need time – perhaps lots of it – to ease into a woodland niche and settle there. Beetles which chew old and decaying wood; birds which use tree holes for nesting; slow-growing lichens, liverworts and mosses which take many years to establish on trunk or stem, or which need moisture and cool shade to sustain them – these are some of the missing links in a coppice which can be forged in old woodlands elsewhere.

The richest places for such wildlife are long-established wood pastures, such as former Royal Forests, created as human preserves for the pursuit of deer, and medieval deer parks, formerly used to give winter supplies of fresh meat from the animals confined by their boundary palings. Within the old deer parks, the original tree-huggers – plants which cling to trunks or sprout and dangle from branches – can literally find their true niche and proliferate.

Opposite: Primroses and bluebells under coppiced sycamore stools.

A ranger in the Dalkeith Country Park, Edinburgh, shows two interested visitors some bugs from ancient trees.

For these 'epiphytes', the contrast between copse and old pasture woodland can be extreme. Coppicing may have miracle-grow properties for spring flowers, summer warblers, and many invertebrates, but it cuts off the scope for other species even before they have taken hold, let alone reached their prime.

No one wood can be all things to all wildlife: good woods for lichens are not necessarily good for mosses, just as butterfly-rich woods and those crawling with click beetles have different characteristics. So promotion of diversity of life in these places needs broadscale planning and collection of information, as well as careful action (or no action at all, save for letting things be) in particular woods.

Coppicing is seldom a big earner nowadays, especially in the years of re-establishing a rotation in an abandoned copse. But it is feasible, given a supply of volunteer labour, or in some places a local market for products such as hurdles and bean poles. Charcoal burning kilns are appearing in some woodlands again, as are heavy horses. Once decried as inefficient timber-shifters compared with machines, big horses are now proving their worth as precision movers of logs in woods which would otherwise be damaged by the access tracks needed for machinery to operate.

This gradual resurgence of old skills, helped by new knowledge, is one reflection of a changing attitude to woodlands. The spread of new woods planted with locally appropriate trees, which have great amenity and wildlife value, is another. This includes woods being established in regionwide projects in areas such as central Scotland and the Midlands. These hold the promise of bringing trees and people back together, with woods as a part of the natural fabric, in some of the most densely populated areas of Britain.

But the clearest expression of an altered way of looking at the woods in recent years has come through the sheer passion of response to schemes which threaten destruction of much valued woods. Most celebrated of these causes has been that of Oxleas Wood, London's largest surviving fragment of ancient woodland, which faced the prospect of an unceremonious carve-up by chainsaw and bulldozer to make way for a proposed east London river crossing in the early 1990s. A Department of Transport plan – to push a 120-metre-wide cutting through Oxleas, felling hundreds of oaks, hornbeams and sweet chestnuts and driving a wedge of traffic pollution and noise into its heart – met fierce opposition.

Purchased by public subscription many decades ago, declared a Site of Special Scientific Interest in 1984 and now within the care of the Borough of Greenwich, Oxleas Wood is important to many kinds of people. Locals who value it as a place to visit, other Londoners who cherish its part in the city's history, naturalists who enjoy its birds and other creatures, conservationists from both near and far, concerned to see Britain's obligations to protect important wildlife refuges upheld – all these and more rallied to oppose the scheme.

It was a long battle, but the success of the campaign by Oxleas' defenders struck an important chord. For whatever its ramifications in terms of government transport policies, adherence to European Union conservation statutes, and other such matters, it indicated one thing very clearly – that trees had been restored, for this community, in this place, to a position of real importance in local life.

That chord now echoes in many other woods, in many other places. Part of its resonance comes from the resurgence of activities in both old woods and new; part in the activism which has seen wood after wood defended against destruction, (although not often as successfully as at Oxleas, as the bitter conflict over ancient woodland felled in the path of the Newbury Bypass showed in 1996). Part is simply in the rediscovery of woods and trees as important elements in daily life – whether they be plane trees on a London street, or small-leaved limes in an ancient copse.

It is a dramatic turnaround from the obsession with monoculture forestry which, for several decades, was a dominant feature of British and Irish dealings with trees. Mega-scale conifer forestry is still to the fore, but now has enormous potential (being realised, in part, through many schemes promoted by both Forest Enterprise and the Forestry Authority, the two wings of the current Forestry Commission) for modification to a more benign presence. As stands mature, a variety of species and tree ages can be introduced to plantations.

The widespread appreciation of trees and their value is a rising force, and it is one which can fuse fresh ideas with well-tried skills to give new routes back into the woods. It is a process which is fostering deep connections with the groves which so nearly were lost, and the many others that are now in the making.

Opposite: Broad buckler fern, dog's mercury and wild garlic in ancient woodland.

SNOWS IN HIGH SUMMER

From the low ground near the river, reaching the summit was a tantalizing notion – a challenge to take up most of the day. The mountain bulk, rising soft-shouldered and rounded above forest and moor, seemed a benign presence, inviting closer acquaintance.

One thousand metres higher, the cover of heather and other dwarf shrubs is giving way underfoot to increasing bareness of frost-shattered stone, and the prospect is altogether different. Now, the backward view has most allure – down to the great swathe of bottle-green pine forest below, and out over the plain where a loch winks reflected sunlight from cool water.

Above, the ramp of hill seems endless. This landscape has monumental proportions, but perception of it progressively narrows to smaller and smaller, self-centred details. An ache of muscles in the upper calves, the sting of chill air on straining lungs, the image of one walking boot, then the other, rising and falling in ascent towards an unseen goal.

Today, the concentration of will-power pays off. Another few hundred metres, a final heave of effort, and the tiredness evaporates with a dramatic change of scene. Up on the summit plateau, the view is broad once more, taking in a huge sweep of ground – a high tableland of crumbled rock and small clumps of plants, its finest details seeming sharply etched in light of astonishing clarity. Beyond the immediate surface, mountain top after mountain top grades in a progression of hazy tones towards far horizons.

The snow patch by the summit is the icing on this high-level slice, something to cool face and arms on a July afternoon. But the main tingle is all around; a beauty so simple and yet so mirage-like that it eludes any easy description. I recall the words of the writer Nan Shepherd, who knew this place well as a retreat from a 'disturbed and uncertain world' below, in the closing years of the Second World War. 'One never quite knows the mountain,' she wrote, 'nor oneself in relation to it. However often I walk on them, these hills hold astonishment for me. There is no getting accustomed to them.'

A change in the wind, a lengthening of shadows, and a mass of storm cloud gathering in the west; the mountain mood changes, seems suddenly threatening. People have died of exposure here, even in summer. Time to descend before the rain sets in, accepting the inevitability of another all too brief encounter with the highest lands, yet hungering for more.

From one perspective, the mountain areas of Britain and Ireland are molehills in an international context. Ground over 600 metres above sea level covers not much more than half a million hectares in Britain, and a mere 24,000 hectares in Ireland. Real high-altitude land – around the somehow mystic figure (from the point of view of many hillwalkers) of 3,000 feet or more, in imperial measurement, or just over 900 metres in metric, covers barely 40,000 hectares of Britain (mostly in Scotland), and scarcely any of Ireland.

South of the Scottish Highlands, many hills are modest. England's rocky Pennine spine eases fractionally above 600 metres in the rounded hills of the Peak District, and pushes a little higher in the north. The very highest point in England – Scafell, in the Lake District – falls short of 1,000 metres. Wales has a cluster of peaks topping this figure in Snowdonia, and Ireland manages to reach 1,041 metres at Carrantouhill in the midst of the deliciously named MacGillicuddy's Reeks.

But the eagle's share of mountain ground above 900 metres in Britain and Ireland (about 90 per cent of it) lies in Scotland, beyond the Boundary Fault which draws such a clear divide between the lowlands of Scotland's central plain and the highland ground beyond. Even here, the peak altitude – of 1,347 metres on Ben Nevis – is no giddy height on a Himalayan or even Alpine scale. But simple comparisons of such bald statistics belie the special nature and importance of these ranges on Europe's western fringe.

For the extreme climatic gradients on British and Irish hills, coupled with the oceanic influence of rain-laden winds, give them a special place in the global mountain picture. Modest heights they may be, but they have a peculiar intensity of living conditions, given a distinctive regional cachet by the ocean air.

Never mind the summit cairn, feel the rise. What they lack in overall stature, the British mountains, especially, can make up for in sheer rate of change from valley to top. The fall-off in temperature with increasing height – about 1° Celsius for every 150 metres climbed – is one of the sharpest in the world. The British uplands are also one of the windiest parts of the planet.

At an altitude of 857 metres at Great Dunfell in Cumbria, for example, the average daily wind speed tops 10 metres a second, or gale force six (enough to give a stormy crossing for a boat at sea level) on one day in three, while gusts of twice that strength are common, both here and in many upland places. A long run of windspeed readings, made at the observatory on Ben Nevis at the end of last century, logged an average of 261 gales a year there.

Alongside the plummeting temperatures and blustering winds, come clouds carrying rain and snow. Sunshine dims as cloudiness rises, then bursts through again at the very highest levels. Maps of precipitation (showing both rain and snowfall) and relief (displaying height above sea level), show close overlap in these islands, with the greatest precipitation on some of the highest ground. Lee slopes tend to be wetter than peaks, but the difference between

Opposite: A golden eagle feeding on a mountain hare in the Scottish Highlands.

low ground and high in the same area can be astonishing.

At 2 metres average annual rainfall, Fort William is hardly a prime spot for sun-seekers, but even that downpouring pales in comparison to the 4 metres of snow and rain dumped each year on Ben Nevis beyond. In Ireland, the higher peaks attract a Fort William-scale libation from the heavens of twice that showered on the central plain.

Cold air streaming down from the Arctic in northerlies, or sweeping east across the north sea from the continent, can be a powerful snowmaker when it hits eastern hills. This can happen at any season, but the snow lie is often fleeting, both here and further west. The interplay of warm airflows from the Atlantic with the chillier, snow-boosting draughts sees to that, sometimes melting an upland blanket-load of snow within hours, pushing spate rivers fed by meltwater to the brim and beyond, and testing lowland flood defences to destruction. The winds that brought the snow can also blast it skywards and away.

Other air movements can bring coolness down from the heights. At evening, when a high plateau's surface temperature drops to less than that of the air above an adjacent valley, the colder, denser air slides down the valleyside in a 'catabatic' wind – like a chilly exhalation from the mountain as the sun sets, spreading its influence to settlements below. Close to, whether huddled in a village at their skirts, or perched lofty and exposed on windy ridges, the mountains are a powerful presence, drawing in clouds, working the weather, dominating the landscape, tantalizing with their lumpen bulk, and amazing with their scope for changed perspectives and special challenges.

Each country in Britain and Ireland has places such as these, which can work their spell on the region around them and draw-in visitors from far beyond, keen to have a brush with some mountain magic. In Wales, Snowdon and its attendant peaks have the strongest pull. There is good rock for climbers here – including faces and slopes used as training ground for Sir John Hunt's team before the first ascent of Everest in 1953.

By contrast, the century-old rack and pinion railway, which runs up Snowdon from Llanberis, can give passengers an easy ascent of the highest peak south of Scotland, then rattle them down again in time for tea. It is an experience which seems somehow at odds with the scale of the place, yet for millions of people over the years of its operation, the railway may have provided a once-in-a-lifetime trip to an Alpine-level top.

Away from the main tourist routes in Snowdonia, a hiker with an eye for plants might see tufted saxifrage, arctic mouse-ear, northern rockcress or Alpine woodsia at their only locations south of the Highlands, or hope for an encounter with the rare Snowdon lily, confined in Britain to a few cliffs in the area. Not that far away as the raven flies, the hills of the Lake District, seat of England's loftiest peaks, could offer alpine lady's mantle at its southern British limits, or yellow saxifrages, abundant here, but strangely absent from Snowdonia.

Ascending the Lake District fells gives a cultural shock to anyone more used to the relative quietness of hills in Ireland or Scotland. Here, as in the most popular parts of the even more heavily touristed Peak District (most visited National Park in the world after Mount Fuji in Japan), routes up the mountains are well worn, obvious and often busy with people. A climb can offer the chance to exchange small talk with many different walkers encountered on the broad hill tracks, while the scene at summits can have a foreground filled with a throng of hikers, most sporting colourful day-sacks, anoraks and other gear, much of it made from high-tech fabrics which could perform as well on Everest as in Cumbria.

As on Snowdon, scenes like these challenge easy assumptions about the mountains, for solitary contemplation is not often an option on the Lakeland fells. But there is no denying the enjoyment which huge numbers of walkers gain from a ramble on such heavily-visited hills (or the abiding pleasure which Wainwright's lovingly crafted drawings and descriptions can give them), and that they can achieve this as part of an activity which, at first glance, can appear to be a communal event.

Yet, even on a trail not far from other walkers, the mountains can work wonders with perception, shifting the focus both narrowly on oneself – to the mechanics of the aches and strains of upward progress – then broadening it on the high-level ridges and flats into something utterly different. It could be a view which takes in several counties at a glance; it could be no view at all – a wall of greyness, the shifting mist pressing in, obscuring all sense of distance save for the niggling, sometimes frightening, thought that the edge is close by – and beyond that, oblivion.

Such perception may be altered in some of its details by the proximity of other people, but its fundamentals remain potent – a frisson to remember for a long time to come; a sense of wildness, and of one's position in relation to that wildness. In other words, these places offer the chance of an encounter with wilderness – for wilderness is as much a state of mind as it is a state of place.

In Ireland, the mountain wilds are relatively few, with the major masses clumped in the west. The Reeks and the Brandon and Slieve Mish ranges in Kerry, the Twelve Bens in Connemara and the Derryveagh mountains in Donegal, take in much of the high-level western ground, with the Mournes in County Down and the Wicklow mountains south of Dublin as the highest hills of the east.

What they lack in quantity (despite the Irish tendency to name even the most modest of hills 'Mount'), the true Irish mountains make up for in their qualities of spaciousness, coupled (by English and Welsh standards) with a general lack of people pressure. The tops can be soggy, and notable more for mosses and liverworts than for scarce mountain blooms, but there is still scope for a brush with some ice age relics in a few places, such as the Ben Bulben range in Sligo, where some true mountain plants cling to the cliffs and screes.

Scotland is different again. Seen from the low hills perched on the faultline at the fringe of the Trossachs, the mountains beyond stretch northwards in a seemingly endless corrugation of gneiss and granite. Some of these peaks are hotspots for walkers – not least the 'Munros'.

Opposite: Llyn Bochllwyd and Tryfan in the Snowdonia National Park, winter.

Walkers and climbers abound in the Snowdonia National Park.

Sir Hugh Thomas Munro was a founding member and early president of the Scottish Mountaineering Club. His 'Tables of Heights Over 3,000 Feet', published in the first issue of the SMC journal in 1891, has in much more recent years become the stimulus for legions of 'Munro-baggers', intent on ascending every summit on Munro's list. Some take things further, aiming for winter ascents, running ascents and the like. With all this frenzied and sometimes obsessive activity focused on his modest tables, there is a certain irony in the fact that Munro himself did not manage to climb every peak on his list, remaining two short at the time of his death in 1919.

Even with this burgeoning of Munro-bagging as a pastime, many of the major Scottish hills are relatively quiet – places which offer genuine scope for recreation and contemplation away from a press of people. With such an abundance of high ground available, it may seem surprising that passions still run high about people-linked problems in some Scottish mountain areas.

This applies especially to the Cairngorms, where conflict over the use of the mountain ground, and possible ways to protect it, has raged hot and impassioned for decades. But, for good or ill, the Cairngorms is an area which seems to merit full-bodied feeling. The mountains, moors, woods, rivers, glens and straths of the Cairngorms are Britain and Ireland's upland supersystem. The massif at the core, formed some 400 million years ago

from red granite squeezed into being at the roots of an Alpine-scale range, which once stretched from what is now Scotland to Scandinavia, holds the greatest expanse of ground over 900 metres in these islands.

Nowhere else in the world, save for Baffin Island in arctic Canada, is there such a wide range of landforms in such a small area. Ancient tors moulded eons ago in desert conditions much nearer the equator, plateaux heaved up in continental birth spasms, corries scooped out by glaciers, and lochans spawned from chips off the old ice age blocks, lie near snowbeds which still linger through most summers. It is like part of the Arctic which has broken free, drifted south, and lodged in Scotland's mountainous heart.

The wildlife emphasises such a link even further, with a range of plants, insects and birds found here and on continental mountains, but in few or any other parts of Britain and Ireland. Birds such as the dotterel – a dapper wader which uses tundra-like barrens as its breeding place – and the snow buntings which swirl their piebald plumage like spindrift over the high Cairngorms throughout the year, attract much of the limelight in publicity about these heights.

Plant cover can also give striking parallels with other countries, especially Norway. Beyond the Cairngorms, it is often difficult – due to centuries of modification by grazing and other human-linked influences – to find the clear changes of vegetation type which give a visible sign of increasingly harsh living conditions on a mountain ascent. But in the Cairngorms, such a journey through different life-zones is still possible.

So it is not surprising that debate about the use of these mountains, especially for downhill skiing and its necessary paraphernalia, can be characterized as an argument between those who hope for the preservation of such natural qualities, and others who reckon that a little space given over to mechanized recreation is no threat to the wider scene. Nowhere else in Britain and Ireland has such argument been more polarized than in the Cairngorms, especially in relation to successive plans for downhill skiing upon the slopes of the eponymous mountain.

Downhill skiing, helped by tows and chairlifts, began here in the 1960s. Every few years since the early 1980s, the Cairngorm Chairlift Company has proposed schemes for expansion and re-development. Two of them involved plans to gain access to Lurcher's Gully – a small place which now has a big international reputation – and the latest includes proposals to run a railway from the ski area car parks to a visitor centre within a short walk from the very summit of Cairngorm. At each stage, these plans have been bitterly contested, latterly by consortiums of conservation, mountaineering and access groups (one of which coalitions it was my privilege to chair in the late 1980s).

At the time of a second public inquiry into the proposals (later rejected) for Lurcher's Gully, the then Secretary of State for Scotland received one of the largest mailbags ever

Opposite: Moss Campion, an Arctic-Alpine plant, in the Cwm Idwal National Nature Reserve in Snowdonia.

sent to the Scottish Office on a planning issue. Many of these letters were from people living far beyond the mountains, many others were from Highland residents.

For this was, and is, no simple conflict, typically (and wrongly) characterized by headline writers as 'conservation versus jobs'. The alignment of so many kinds of groups agin it, and the concerns of a fair proportion local folk, should testify to that. It is something with a wider and more complex resonance, revealed in part by the concerns of people living far removed from the slopes of contention.

Heavily visited the Cairngorms may be, but as the Lake District fells demonstrate, well-trodden mountains can have a value of perceived wildness which is rare indeed. Wordsworth fretted over this at the time of proposals for the construction of the Kendal and Windermere railway. 'Is then no nook of English ground secure from rash assault?' runs the most famous line of his 1844 sonnet against the scheme, often quoted since then by people bothered by potential changes in other much-loved landscapes.

But Wordsworth was unashamedly elitist, arguing that the beauty of the Lakes was, essentially and permanently, a minority taste, which could only be savoured by people with the necessary education, cultivated sensibilities and leisure time to appreciate it. Even if taking a less extreme viewpoint, a paradox persists. For if the very things that can make a landscape beautiful and inspirational are those that can be obliterated by human pressure, then providing ever-easier access to them risks loving them to death.

But the paradox, perhaps, is imperfect. For the lure of the mountains comes both through their outward appearance and through their impact on thought. Just over a ridge, within a few hundred metres of the main ski runs of Cairngorm, it is possible to walk under corries where the ice climbing can be superb, past a snowfield which avalanches in summer, over alpine shrubs and frost-heaved pebbles, and up, along the lip of a dizzying gorge, to a plateau where ptarmigan and other snowbirds call. It could be the Arctic, but it is Scotland. It could be far removed from human artifacts, but it is not. The nub is in the perception.

This scenario suggests that, if decision making about the highest ground accepts variety of use, and accepts the near-inevitability of big visitor numbers in some areas while maintaining features that keep others remote, and does not allow single recreational interests to dominate whole mountains – then some balance can be achieved.

In 1901, John Muir - ex-patriot Scot and prime mover in the establishment of National Parks in the USA – wrote that: 'Thousands of tired, nerve-shattered, over-civilized people are beginning to find out that going to the mountains is going home.'

Nearly a century later, his words still seem to ring true among the rock walls of the high corries in his homeland. But their challenge has never been greater.

Right: Ski runs adjacent to the Northern Corries in the Cairngorm Mountains, Inverness-shire.

Far Right: Looking down the Chalamain Gap, Cairngorms, over Glen More to Abernethy.

A BLAZE OF WHINS

Linked by ling and divided by vinegar, coconut and salt, the three principal types of heathland in Britain and Ireland have both common threads and separate slants. Purple and pink are the dominant tones in their weave of vegetation in late summer, principally through ling and other heaths and heathers which lend their name to such places.

But different emphases of colour, pattern and scent, related to variations in plant mix, soil and climate, give a tang to regional heathland airs that can help to distinguish each from the others, even without taking their pronounced geographical separation into account. All have been helped to spread in the past by human enterprise, principally through controlled grazing of domestic stock in the lowlands and coastlands, and by burning in the uplands. All are now much reduced after more than two centuries of shifting agricultural patterns and the rise in conifer-based forestry, as well as encroachment from other types of land use.

Most widespread of the remaining heaths are the upland ones – the places usually known simply as 'moorlands' – often created and maintained, through the rotational burning of heather, to boost populations of red grouse for shooting (see 'Purple Passage'). These thrive on acidic soils over ancient rocks, in hilly areas where rainfall can be heavy. It is as if there is a dash of vinegar in the peaty water that helps to sustain them, under skies that are seldom cloudless, and where massive swathes of ling spread their purple haze in summer.

Maritime heaths cling to some of the western and northern fringes – capping the upper edges of cliffy coasts in parts of Scotland, south-west England, Wales and Ireland which are often exposed to gales and sea spray. The perennial green of stiff-leaved crowberry plants, suffused by the ephemeral, powder blue of squill in late spring, the pinks of thrift, heath and bell heather flowers in summer, and hung with shiny black berries in autumn, gives some of the seasonal tone to these seaboard heaths.

Wave-splash and windy weather do the main shaping here, pushing tough plants down close to the thin soil, and adding a sprinkle of saltiness to their soft petals and hard leaves. But nibbling by cattle and sheep can keep them in trim, favouring woody shrubs and flowers, which thrive in short turf, over the more palatable grasses which would otherwise invade. The close crop is good for other wildlife too, and without it, a bird like the chough – that extrovert and raucous tumbler of some coastal updraughts – could be floored.

The lowland heaths often come with a whiff of coconut, wafted out when the sun's warmth coaxes perfume from masses of gorse flowers above sandy land where patches of ling may mix with bracken, grasses or bare soil in a mosaic more varied than in the other heathland types. Now reduced almost entirely to small fragments of their former extent, and confined mainly to pockets in southern England and East Anglia, these places still hold bright flakes of past glory.

Some of the rarest creatures in Britain cling-on as residents here, adding exotic touches to the heathland sounds and colours, from the sweet-noted ululation of woodlark song and the harsh rattle of natterjack toad calls, to the *vin rouge* of a Dartford warbler's chest and the hot greens of a male sand lizard's skin. The cool-blooded can warm-up here, so the lowland heaths are havens for dragonflies and many other insects, and for reptiles (all six British representatives of which live in them). Some warm-blooded creatures and sun-loving plants, more at home in Mediterranean temperatures, may tolerate their conditions in average years, but risk population crashes in times of chill.

Other remnants of lowland heath still survive on the western and northern fringes of Iberia and France, in Germany, the Low Countries and southern Scandinavia. The 47,000 hectares or so that remains in England is a relatively small expanse of ground, comprising

---

Opposite: Bell heather carpets the lowland heath at Thursley Common National Nature Reserve in Surrey.

Below: Housing development threatens Canford Heath SSSI in Dorset.

hundreds of shrunken patches. But even this modest spread makes England the lowland heath capital of the planet, with more than a third of the total area in Europe. Almost all of the English remnants lie south of a line from the northern shore of the Wash to the Severn Estuary, with a few outliers beyond this, the most substantial of which is Cannock Chase.

The major concentration, totalling more than 26,000 hectares, is in Hampshire and Dorset, most strikingly in the New Forest, (now the finest example of a grazed heathland complex anywhere in Western Europe) and in coastal heaths such as Arne. Elsewhere, the other principal areas which still harbour such heaths are in the grassy, steppe-like Brecklands at the borders of Norfolk and Suffolk, the 'Sandlings' near the Suffolk coast, in Surrey and in the West Country, especially Cornwall.

Substantial chunks of these heaths owe their survival to the common land status of the ground which supports them. Because no single owner has held absolute sway in decisions about their use, they have persisted when many other tracts, not held in common as community grazings, have long ago gone under the plough, conifer plantation or housing estate. Classic heathland commons include stretches at Thursley and Frensham, and much of the New Forest, whose fate is determined by its unique, ancient and complex legislation.

'Kissing's out of season when the gorse is out of bloom,' goes the saying, or variations of

---

Bell heather, western gorse and Cornish heath on typical Cornish heathland on The Lizard.

it, in many parts of the country where this spikey shrub grows, for there is seldom a time when you can't find a flower, or at least a swelling bud, on a bush or two. By that token, lowland heaths must have been a snogger's paradise in times past, for different types of gorse – from the widespread European, to the more localized western and dwarf furzes, do well in their acid, free-draining soils.

Gorse can survive brief fire, pushing up new shoots from unburnt bases of stems, and tolerate some nibbling. In the past, gorse was valued as a source of winter fodder, either crushed for use by a variety of stock, or through young growth consumed on site by cattle and ponies. Cut and bundled, it could also be used as fuel in ovens and kilns.

Nowadays, the perceived value of gorse comes more from its role as shelter for scarce nesting birds and reptiles, and the fact that it harbours a larger number of invertebrates than heather. But it can also become a problem if the brake of grazing is released, spreading fast and smothering other vegetation in an impenetrable monoculture.

The Dartford warbler is one species whose British dwellings are now almost exclusively in dry lowland heaths where there is ample (but not rampant) gorse. A male on a gorse spray, resplendent in grey and pink breeding finery, throat puffed as he spills out an atonal jumble of song, is a potent symbol of the southern heaths.

But the Dartford warbler has come perilously close to losing its grip on England altogether in recent decades. Cold winters can kill four in every five of them; (it is reckoned that a mere eleven pairs survived the hard winters of the early 1960s). So further pressure, from removal of their preferred nesting sites in deep heather and gorse, can add insult to injury. Despite such setbacks, the British population is now easing close to 1,000 pairs. This is small beer by continental standards, but the best local tally for more than half a century.

The woodlark is even rarer. Now confined mainly to Devon, the New Forest, the Hampshire/Surrey border, Breckland and part of the Suffolk coast, its range has shrunk in the past 30 years, leaving isolated populations, whose combined breeding strength, at the last estimate, is a mere 350 pairs.

For all the heathland woodlarks, reduction of bare ground and short vegetation (which they need for food gathering), has put a progressive squeeze on their range. A principal cause of this loss, (aside from the complete destruction of heaths) has been the steady upsurge and spread of grasses, shrubs and trees on many lowland heaths, following the reduction or complete removal of grazing.

Therein hangs a tale or two. For grazing has been a boon to lowland heaths in the past, as its loss is a bane in the present. Over 8,000 years ago, the areas which became prime heathland were largely covered by woods of lime, hazel and oak. Major clearance of this woodland began in earnest in Neolithic and Bronze Age times.

Once the trees were removed, introduction of grazing on the vegetation covering the nutrient-poor soils fostered tough plants, such as heather and gorse. Rapid drainage of the

---

Opposite: A New Forest pony grazing newly-burned heathland.

ree-shorn ground tipped the balance even more in their favour, by leaching away plant boosters, such as lime, magnesium and nitrates, and so increasing acidity and reducing fertility – the kind of conditions in which heathland shrubs can thrive while softer vegetation falters.

To coin some franglais, grazing could then deliver a coup de grass, with domestic stock further weakening the competition, such as grass and young trees, and holding other potential heathland smotherers, such as bracken and gorse, in check. With such forces working in their favour, the lowland heaths grew from small beginnings to become mighty elements in some southern scenes.

Hardy's Egdon, based on experience of huge tracts of Dorset linglands, has become a byword for such lost landscapes. But the resonance of the heaths comes not just from their former scale, but also from their association with freedom – a linkage encouraged, in part, by the common land status and free access of some notable heaths, coupled with their spaciousness. Lands ideally open to all, unfenced, and with views over great carpets of varied colour that take the breath away – no wonder the sense of loss engendered by the heaths can be a sore one for those with an inkling of what went before.

The high roll of good fortune for the lowland heaths hit problems from the end of the seventeenth century onwards, when changes in farming methods made it possible to cultivate ground of even marginal fertility. Many heathlands became fair game for 'improvement' and vanished under the plough, their disappearance accelerated by a squirearchy that used Enclosure Acts as a tool to suppress commons, and grab more land for private benefit.

Such conversion to farmland has gone on practically ever since, although it reached fever pitch in the decades from World War Two until the 1980s. Direct losses also came in other ways, as heaths were swallowed by burgeoning towns and later by forestry. Bournemouth and most of modern Poole, in Dorset, were built on former heathland last century, while the Forestry Commission converted many heaths in the New Forest and elsewhere to conifer plantations during this one.

The statistics of loss, both nationally and for individual counties, show the immensity of change. Between 1800 and the 1980s, the area of lowland heath in England as a whole fell from nearly 200,000 hectares to less than 50,000. In the same period, Breckland lost 85 per

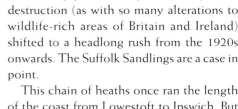

A male natterjack toad calling at night.

cent of its heathland area, Dorset 80 per cent, and Surrey 75 per cent.

Although the changes were well underway in the early part of this period, the pace of destruction (as with so many alterations to wildlife-rich areas of Britain and Ireland) shifted to a headlong rush from the 1920s onwards. The Suffolk Sandlings are a case in point.

This chain of heaths once ran the length of the coast from Lowestoft to Ipswich. But more than 80 per cent of their area disappeared between the 1920s and the 1980s, leaving less than 1,500 hectares, divided between more than 40 separate sites. By the early 1980s, half the former Sandlings area had been ploughed to grow cereals (mainly due to the huge push for increased farm productivity during and after the Second World War). By this time also, one third had been planted with pine trees, while some 15 per cent had been swallowed by new housing, sand and gravel extraction, golf courses and industry. Rapid spread of bracken, birch and pines, unchecked by grazing, was threatening much of what remained.

It was a far cry from the early years of the nineteenth century, when the Aldeburgh poet, George Crabbe, could write:

> Stray over the heath in all its purple bloom-
> And pick the blossom where the wild bees hum:
> And through the broomy Bound with ease they pass
> And press the sandy sheep-walk's slender grass
> Where dwarfish flowers among the gorse are spread
> And the Lamb browses by the Linnet's bed.

Such themes of loss, fragmentation and continuing pressure on surviving remnants can be repeated for county after county, including the heath heartlands such as Dorset. In Hardy's time, heathland cloaked about one eighth of the entire county, spread luxuriantly in a few large tracts. Now, only 5,000 hectares or so remain, split up into more than 150 different patches. The coat of many colours is tattered, and hangs together by the thinnest of threads.

But whereas the story up to recent years is gloomy, the outlook for the future now seems much more colourful, as a brief catalogue of some recent achievements can show. In the

Sandlings, work by a consortium of conservation bodies and local authorities, led by the Suffolk Wildlife Trust, helped to push bracken and trees back from the majority of surviving heaths in the 1980s. A flock of speckled-face Beulah sheep, run by the Suffolk Wildlife Trust, is now helping to keep the ground gained by that push as heathland.

In the Brecks, a decade of effort by English Nature and its predecessor at Brettenham Heath National Nature Reserve has changed large areas of ground, once completely covered by bracken, to open, grassy heathland again, with good re-growth of heather. In Hampshire, resumption of grazing by cattle on Passfield Common has broken up tough tussocks of purple moor grass, dispersed leaf litter to create gaps for heathland plants to colonise, reduced bracken and kept invasion of seedlings from surrounding woodlands at bay.

And in Dorset, large stands of mature pine have been removed from Holton Heath National Nature Reserve, allowing many hectares of heathland to re-establish. Since the area of conifer plantation on heathland soils in Dorset is slightly greater than the area of surviving heathland fragments, the potential for restoration is enormous.

This is the theme also being taken up by the RSPB in Suffolk, through gradual conversion of former agricultural land back to lowland heath beside the Minsmere reserve. It is an interesting turning of the tables in the light of changes in the past few decades.

Careful deployment of livestock can be part of this process in many counties. In northeast Hampshire, where a heathland conservation project has been running for several years, for example, cattle have been the most effective chompers of invading birch trees, since they can kill stumps within a single season. Small breeds, such as Highland, Angus and even Jersey cattle have been doing a good job here. Elsewhere, rare breeds of livestock are enjoying a new lease of popularity as expert restorers of lost heathland splendour.

Techniques such as felling, ground preparation, leaf litter removal and carefully targetted grazing are labour-intensive. It may appear to some like a sort of broad-brush gardening activity, perhaps at odds with the image of the heaths as wild, free and unconstrained by people. But given the history of extensive lowlands heaths, as places which were expanded, maintained and then reduced by the action of people, there is nothing alien about the concept of human intervention here. What was taken away can be restored again, at least in part, by carefully directed action, now backed-up by a wealth of ecological information about the patterns of existence of different forms of heathland life.

Many scarce species, including plants, insects, reptiles, amphibians and birds, stand to benefit from the continuing efforts to rejuvenate the lowland heaths. The natterjack toad is one of these, even though it has all but vanished from its heathland breeding places.

Rarest of the British amphibians, the natterjack has gone from three-quarters of the places where it bred early this century, including all but one of its more than 50 former heathland haunts. The rattling chorus of natterjack males in full song is now something to listen out

Part of the RSPB's reserve at Minsmere in Suffolk is a classic example of lowland heath.

for almost exclusively as a coastal sound on spring and summer nights, on the dune systems from the Wirral to Dumfries (the last strongholds of the British population) or on a very few dunes in western Ireland.

The natterjack has been virtually wiped off the English heathland map by a triple whammy of human-linked blows. Straightforward loss of heathland is the most obvious of these. But souring of water from the acid rain of atmospheric pollution has made many heathland ponds unsuitable for its eggs and tadpoles. Finally, the heightening of vegetation and spread of trees on ungrazed heaths has acted against it too, by transforming the open, warm conditions where it thrives to shadier regimes, more to the liking of the earlier-breeding frogs and common toads.

Once these move in, the natterjack's time in a heathland pool is usually up, for the tadpoles of commoner species can gobble up the natterjack spawn, and so demolish any chance of a local population's survival. But removal of encroaching trees, as has been done near the one remaining natterjack site on a Hampshire heath, can turn things back more in the natterjack's favour.

This recent work has helped natterjack numbers to increase there again, and it has also been a boon to woodlarks. It is a far cry from the time when the chorus of 'Thursley thrushes' as natterjacks were once called in Surrey, could tremble the night air at dozens of places from there to the West Country, but it is a start.

Percussive toads and melodious woodlarks, with extra nightjar churring as a backwash; this is one restoration with more than a hint of the exotic about it. And that seems as it should be, to thrill the coconut-drenched air in these places of sun glint, sand warmth, rarity and space.

Coastal heath at St. David's Head in the Pembrokeshire National Park.

PURPLE PASSAGE

Early autumn is the time, purple the colour. It's the culmination of a process which starts in summer with the pale salmon tints of cross-leaved heath and flushes deep pink when bell heather blooms. It ends with the tinting of the ling – the commonest small woody shrub of British and Irish moors, and the one most people know simply as 'heather'. Each phase runs into the next in a long, slow blush which starts in the south and spreads north, then lingers for weeks on each moor before flowerheads fade in an afterglow of seeding.

The petal colours that launched a billion shortbread tins, from flowers sweet with nectar and delicate with scent, conceal black twigs that crunch underfoot and scratch the legs. 'Go back, go back!' call the grouse, complaining as they retreat in a whirr of flight. Gunfire from thousands of shotguns echoes from dale and glen in answer to their challenge every August, from the 12th and onwards until December in some places, but mostly in the first few weeks of autumn.

Bodies thud to earth, there to be sniffed-out and retrieved by dogs. Feathers, toned deepest russet, black and gold to mirror the season, float briefly in their final blaze of glory, then fall. The carcases may fetch handsome prices in restaurants far from the moors, where city dwellers will dine on the dark, dense meat.

Robert Burns felt the power of such contrasts, and crystallized one of the contradictions:

. . . 'Now westlin winds and slaught'ring guns
Bring Autumn's pleasant weather;
The moorcock springs on whirring wings
Amang the blooming heather'.

More than two centuries later, I recollect the words as I stand up to the knees in flowering ling, listening to the grouse call, watching an irridescent green tiger beetle on a stem – a biting emerald in the shrubbery. Around and below it, the leaves of blaeberry (or bilberry, or whortleberry, or what you will) are also beginning to show their autumn colours, in pigments red as fire, or blood.

Moorland dominated by ling is found only near the western seaboard of Europe, with its finest, most expansive domains in north-eastern Britain. It does best on fairly free-draining, gently sloping, acid soils; in places where the air is often heavy with moisture from rain clouds or sea mist, and trees are few. But it can cope with a wide range of conditions.

It fares well in the drier parts of the western and northern boglands, can tolerate heat in the lowland heaths (see 'A Blaze of Whins') and mountain chill, and is larger and taller than most of the other woody shrubs which often grow alongside it. It can also change its size

and shape to suit local conditions. Plants at high altitude hug the ground with densely inter-twined stems, seeming a race apart from the upright, branching ling of the valley sides and bog hummocks.

This is the plant which can fuel the uplands, providing year-round food for grazers like red deer, mountain hares and sheep, and for smaller nibblers, such as caterpillars and beetles, that munch its tiny leaves. Moors cloaked in it are the preferred dwelling place for several kinds of birds. Red grouse, hen harrier, merlin and golden plover like nothing better; golden eagles and peregrines can benefit from a dash of it in their territories, giving the option of good hunting over open ground.

In the natural course of things, heather is a plant of woodland clearings – part of the succession of different kinds of vegetation which moves in to cover ground bared by fire or exposed to extra light by windthrow of trees – giving an imperial pulse of colour at shrub level before a shift to more dominant greens as the canopy closes. People have been creating new opportunities for it for millennia, by making holes in the forest cover and introducing grazing patterns which can favour heather over grasses and trees.

The tough stems could be put to many different uses. Rope made of twisted heather was found in excavations of the neolithic settlement of Skara Brae on Orkney, while huge balls of heather rope, or 'wisps', were still in use for thatching on Orkney until this century (where heather could also provide the material for the thatch itself). Besom brooms, basket handles, and insulation in cavity walls were some other uses in Scotland, where the technique of making a heather lining for box beds was also developed to a fine art.

According to one writer, this, at its best, required the longest, straightest stalks to be pulled (with as little accompanying root as possible) when the heather was in full bloom. After being spread out like hay to dry for a few hours, the material was packed densely, with all the flowering heads upright and leaning a little towards the head of the bed. Held in by logs at its edges, the finished product looked like a field of purple reclining in a breeze and gave out a honeyed, soporific perfume – a mattress fit for an emperor, which could be created in a peasant's cottage by those in the know.

Burning of heather in strips, each of which will be torched again after ten to fifteen years, is one of the keys to survival of widespread heather on upland moors which has been developed in the last couple of centuries. As heather grows and ages, its stems become thicker, woodier and more gappy, producing poorer quality and reduced amounts of fodder. Crucially, it also loses vigour and is less able to regrow after fire. The trick with good heather maintenance is to weigh such matters in the balance.

Prudent practice – burning not too often and not too hot – removes old stems but keeps

A helicopter spraying bracken to control its spread on a heather moor in the Berwyn Mountains in Powys.

the rootstock alive. These roots can then thrust-up young, nutritious shoots, which have now been released from competition from plants such as birch seedlings – frazzled by the blaze – and which have an excellent nursery bed for their own, plentiful seeds in the scorched earth around them. Out of the flames, a fragile stability can be born, somewhat akin to the effect of repeated coppicing in a lowland broadleaved wood.

Deliberate torching of heather moorland has probably been done in a haphazard way for a very long time. But using fire in a more controlled way, and within narrowly defined limits of hill ground, only spread widely as a heather booster when sheep appeared in force on the upland scene. Even for hardy sheep breeds, such as blackfaces and Cheviots, which can stay out on the hill all year and forage on snow-covered land, heather can be a life-saver, offering a vital source of green food through the thick of winter snows. In Scotland, 'muirburn' spread from the Southern Uplands – an early powerhouse of the north British sheep industry – to the Highlands as sheep farmers homed-in on the clan lands.

Sheep are now a near ubiquitous feature of the Highland hills and glens. But it was only in 1762 that widespread husbandry of flocks began here, when farmers from Annandale moved north to Perthshire and Dunbartonshire and then beyond, bringing their Linton blackfaces and their knowledge of muirburn with them. Leases for the new grazings (many

Opposite: Heather moor on the edge of the Vale of Clwyd, an Area of Outstanding Natural Beauty in Denbighshire.

of which, in the northern Highlands, were on ground from which former tenants had been evicted to make way for the woolly hordes) often specified the amount of moorland (usually about one tenth) which should be burnt in a year.

Muirburn for sheep took in greater swathes of hill than the patchier, smaller-scale burning which eased-in during the nineteenth century as the preferred method of encouraging the productivity of another creature – the red grouse. The fluctuating fortunes of this bird are now so linked with the fate of large, ling-lavished moors as to make the bird and place seem almost synonymous. For 'grouse moor' is very definitely the apposite term for such upland heaths.

A stocky bird, about the size of a bantam hen, the red grouse is an outlier of the circumpolar willow ptarmigan – a kind of superspecies whose various septs and clans can be found from Canada and the Aleutians through Siberia to Scandinavia and on to these western outposts. The British and Irish birds benefit from the fairly mild, oceanic climate here, and are closely hefted to heather, and so to the moors which have been expanded for their benefit.

No other bird in the world makes such heavy use of heather. Young shoots are its staple food, older clumps give cover for nesting and screening from predators. Many red grouse live-out their fairly short lives close to their hatching place. Highly territorial by instinct, each young cock tries to pitch his stall for a monogamous liaison not far from his father's patch. Low-ranking birds which fail to do this tend to move from their home heath and suffer high mortality from predators.

Those that stay can still face major problems, principally through the impact of the disease, louping ill – carried by sheep ticks – which kills chicks, and from infestation of adult birds by a parasite – the strongyle worm. Together with fluctuations in food supply and aspects of the grouse's own social behaviour, such factors can lead to huge changes in grouse numbers on a particular moor. Peak years of great abundance can be followed by troughs of great dearth, in a process which can veer from feast to famine and back again, in cycles of less than a decade.

The red grouse has been on the human hit-list of highly prized quarry species for centuries. Arguably, only a small part of the motivation for this pursuit has been based on the bird's gastronomic potential. Grouse meat is dark and lean when cooked, but is no more distinctive than many other kinds of game; jellied berries, a sauce and the vapours of a fine wine can be its saving grace in many an expensive restaurant.

Rather, the complete reliance of the red grouse on heather has allowed high cost, exclusive activities to grow up around it. Its value to people may lie as much in the scarcity and narrow limits of the ground which it inhabits as in the bird itself. For scarce resources often attract a premium if you can control their sale and use.

The red grouse owes its official status as a gamebird to birds of prey, especially the peregrine falcon. For it was the passion of medieval nobility for falconry and their desire to secure the supply of suitable targets for their cherished birds of the gauntlet which led to

A female red grouse brooding chicks in the Forest of Bowland in Lancashire.

opposed to using the new firepower in a 'driven' grouse shoot: 'I cannot say that my taste leads me to rejoice in the slaughter of a large bag of grouse in one day,' he wrote in the early 1840s. He added that he had 'much more satisfaction in killing a moderate quantity of birds in a wild and varied range of hill, with my single brace of dogs, and wandering in any direction that fancy leads me, than having my day's beat laid out for me, with relays of dogs and keepers, and all the means of killing the grouse on easy walking ground, where they are so numerous that one has only to load and fire.'

In the early nineteenth century, responsibility for muirburn had been transferred from farmers and shepherds to gamekeepers, who at first drastically reduced the extent of fires by burning a mosaic of small patches in a restricted area, to give cover for grouse which could be 'walked up' with dogs. In the 1870s, when it was eventually realised that both sheep and grouse could benefit from similar heather conditions, promoted by regular burning, the patchwork method was expanded to take in a greater proportion of a moorland's surface. From then on, this has been the widely accepted pattern of rejuvenating heather and maintaining a grouse moor for driven shooting.

Despite the qualms of St. John and others, including noble lords who asked questions in parliament about an activity which some of them viewed as 'unsporting', the driven grouse shoot continued in the ascendant, as did the spaces customized to support it. As profits from sheep farming in the uplands tumbled in the 1870s, laid low by a combination of poor productivity on grazings which had been heavily stocked in previous decades and poor competitiveness with foreign imports of meat and wool, so land prices in the uplands became dirt cheap for those with disposable wealth.

By this time, improved roads and railways had made access to upland areas, even those in remote parts of the Highlands, much easier, provided one could afford the fare. Eager to let rip with the latest weaponry, and with bank balances bulging from the profits of industry and trade in the burgeoning empire, some of the most seriously rich people of the day took to the hills and moors. Huge tracts of former sheepwalk were transformed to ground where grouse could be shot and, mainly in Scotland, deer stalked. Another challenging target – the mountain hare, which is almost as reliant on young heather as the grouse – was introduced to North Wales, the Pennines, the Lake District and several Scottish islands, where it briefly expanded its British range and diversified the shooting. But variety was certainly not the order of the Victorian upland day where many other mammals and birds were concerned. Anything with a hooked beak and talons, or claws and jaws which could grab a grouse, became proscribed as 'vermin' by the army of gamekeepers, now well established as custodians of the heather and of the chosen few species deemed fair game for the guns.

The toll taken of birds of prey and carnivores, sometimes recorded in great detail in the gamebooks of the time, was a terrible one. Eagles, buzzards, kites and harriers were drastically reduced. Pine martens were virtually wiped from the map of mainland Britain – pushed to an enclave in the wilds of Sutherland – while wildcats retreated to the rockier-

laws protecting grouse and other 'moorfowl' from general attack. Some of these statutes were draconian, such as one Scottish law of 1551, which threatened the death penalty on anyone killing game with guns, but allowed 'gentlemen with hawks' free rein. In those days, grouse were valued simply as challenging targets which could coax a sterling display of aerobatics from a much-cosseted falcon.

Using guns to kill grouse was well established by the late eighteenth century. But this was done on the move, by walking over a moor in the company of dogs, which could locate the quarry and retrieve corpses after shots had found their mark. In a 'driven' grouse shoot, packs of grouse are flushed by a line of 'beaters' – people moving through the heather with sticks and flags to scare the birds into flight – towards shooters stationed behind low-walled 'butts'. This form of shooting only grew in popularity from the 1840s onwards.

New technology, in the form of the breach-loading shot gun, helped its rise. With its rapid re-arming capabilities, the breach-loader easily outgunned the fiddly old muzzle-loaders, and made fast-moving birds and animals – the more the merrier – the upland targets of choice for those with the wealth or connections to participate.

But some Victorian shooters, including the famous Charles St. John, remained bitterly

Opposite: Heather moorland at Farndale Common in the North Yorkshire Moors National Park.

Grouse hanging in a gamekeeper's larder in the Forest of Bowland.

remoter glens and polecats were laid low. Poisoning, shooting, trapping and snaring became the stock-in-trade of the new grouse guardians, who could now dispatch with impunity birds such as the peregrine, whose harming could have been a capital offence some centuries earlier.

For a few decades, the pay-off on the softly scented killing fields was huge. Released from the checks and balances of the natural predators, and with great swathes of landscape devoted to their mortal needs and convenient dispatch, red grouse thrived, reaching phenomenal densities. In the closing years of the nineteenth century and the early years of this, the best moors could yield bags of 250 grouse shot per square kilometre, with some 100 per square kilometre commonplace.

All the record bags in Britain and Ireland stem from this period. The highest Irish kill – of a few hundred birds in one day at Powerscourt – was in 1890; the highest Scottish and Welsh kills were in 1911 and 1912. But the largest ever was in 1915, as the First World War slid deeper into its four-year mire of carnage. This was the year when Rupert Brooke died in active service on his way to the Dardanelles, when the British offensive on Loos was

Opposite: These sitka spruce plantations are threatening heather moor in Denbighshire.

beaten back with heavy casualties, when John Buchan's 'Thirty Nine Steps' was published, and when, on 12th August, a party of eight guns shot 2,929 grouse on a beat of the Bowland Fells on the western Pennines.

With the literary and military associations of that particular year, and the knowledge of hindsight that another push on the Somme was just months away, it is hard to ignore the double edge of that record-breaking figure. The tension is appropriate, for in the aftermath of that war, things in the uplands, as in every other part of Britain and Ireland, could never be the same again. So great was the mortality of gamekeepers in that hellish conflict that their ranks never regained the levels of their pre-war battalions. The number of game-keepers in Scottish upland estates, for example, is now only some 15 per cent of the early century peak.

The most rapid peacetime changes came on the Irish heaths, where heather is extensive mainly in the Mournes and the Wicklow mountains, and where grouse densities have always been low in comparison to the British mainland. A multiple impact of reduced keepering, the foundation of the Irish Free State, and a consequent rise in absentee land-lordism, reduced the care and maintenance of heather and grouse. Bags dwindled, and by 1945, grouse shooting had all but vanished from the Irish scene.

In Britain, changes have been slower, but the unmistakable trend for both moors and red grouse has been downward for many decades. Here, the area of upland heath has shrunk by one fifth since the 1940s (more in heather heartlands, such as Grampian and Dumfries and Galloway). Large areas of the remainder are in poor shape, being gradually nibbled threadbare by EU-subsidized sheep flocks and with little input of labour to maintain their heather cover. Other parts, including all too many places in north-west Scotland, are ravaged by wanton muirburn. This can often be no more sophisticated in its approach than setting alight to a hillside and watching it blaze, in the hope of coaxing a quick flush of spring grass to feed sheep on the charred ground.

It is a world away, in technique and concept, from the careful conflagration of patches on a grouse moor. But there, the problem now is not too much burning, but too little. The practice has declined for more than forty years, and now only a small proportion of moors is burned on a ten-to-fifteen-year cycle.

In Wales, fewer than one in seven grouse moors is burnt at all, and in England, only about half. Numbers of grouse have also declined, even on moors still actively keepered – albeit by a much diminished workforce. Statistics compiled by the Game Conservancy Trust show that numbers of grouse shot on such moors fell by more than half between the 1920s and the 1980s. And so the story has continued through the 1990s, with years of grouse scarcity on some moors unparalleled in living memory.

Some 450,000 red grouse are shot on Britain's 459 remaining grouse moors each year, including about 250,000 in Scotland, where the kill may support the equivalent of 2,300 full-time jobs. In other words, 110 grouse equals one job. According to the Game Conservancy Trust, driven grouse shooting is only an economic proposition when autumn

Right: A Connemara pony grazing on Diamond Hill moorland area in the Connemara National Park, Eire.

Far Right: Strips of heather are deliberately burned as part of the moorland management process.

grouse numbers top 60 per square kilometre. Many moors now fall below this level.

Such figures can certainly concentrate the minds of those with a vested interest in the heather and its denizens at times, such as recent years, when grouse numbers tumble and profits go into free fall. The usual knock-on which follows means more job losses and more shifts from heather to grassland or trees, including stands of exotic conifers which can swallow great chunks of former moor when the accountants welcome them in.

With its well-documented population cycles, the red grouse has never been an investment for the faint-hearted. It's a bird virtually guaranteed to give a white-knuckle ride for those who wish to reap a steady return from its killing. But the origins of the grouse moors last century, whose rise had as much to do with conspicuous consumption as it did with balancing the books, suggest that a mere profit-and-loss account of the remaining moors is too simplistic an analysis to give a way forward for their future survival.

Thanks to work by several generations of gamekeepers, the North Yorkshire moors, some hills in the Scottish borders and wide swathes of Perthshire and Deeside are now the heatherlands without parallel anywhere else on the planet. These, and other grouse moor strongholds, are also places where a variety of wildlife, such as black grouse, golden plovers, hen harriers, merlins, peregrines, foxes and short-eared owls could potentially thrive.

And there's the rub. For to some people (whose taxes help to subsidize the wider work on upland estates), certain of these species are highly valued members of their country's fauna, while to others (whose work is crucial to the survival of these extensive moors), several of those species may still be viewed as vermin, which eat grouse, grouse eggs and chicks, or disrupt a driven shoot. Reconciliation of such opposing viewpoints seems a tall order. Yet without it, the future of the remaining ling-dominated moors seems shakier than ever.

Perhaps some scope for reconciliation could come from an established source. For lower grouse numbers, living in company with a full complement of other moorland wildlife, seem quite compatible with an earlier style of shooting on the moors.

I turn again to the words of Charles St. John – and ponder the irony as I savour them. This was a man who dispatched a fearsome tally of creatures in his day, yet his talk of moderation, coupled with an appreciation of some of the natural qualities of the hills, seems somehow more in tune with the needs of the present time than does rigid adherence to patterns of moorland activity set later in his century and still haunting the close of this one.

It has been a long, slow fade indeed, but if the purple haze of the world's finest moors is to linger much longer, something radical needs to put a spark back in the heather, kindling conditions for both wildlife and people that suit not just the few, but the many.

Right: Welsh mountain sheep grazing on moorland in Snowdonia National Park.

Opposite: Sharp Tor in Dartmoor National Park, Devon.

CRACKING THE OLD SEA

One afternoon in early summer, I step out from the edge of a small wood. Behind, all is cool, green and intimate – twists of leafy hazel and ash twigs sprouting from short stems above a mossy floor, where pignut, sanicle and orchids snuggle in the dappled shade. Ahead, acre upon acre of greyness.

Bare rock, fissured and cracked, rises glinting to a hill whose naked strata seem to swirl in front of the eyes. I squint at the brightness, dazzled by stone. It feels like the boundary of another planet.

This is the Burren in County Clare, one of the strangest landscapes anywhere, and the largest expanse of 'limestone pavement' in Britain and Ireland. Elsewhere in these islands, the most extensive limestone pavements are in the north of England. The low, wooded hills near Morecambe Bay, sheepwalks riding high on the Pennine flank at Scales Moor on Whernside, Ingleborough and Malham, the rainswept fells around Shap in Cumbria – these are the principal outcrops – with a few smaller patches in Wales, Scotland and the south of Galway. Beyond that, parts of the high Alps and former Jugoslavia hold the other European sites.

Such pavements would be nightmarish for a metropolitan roads department, for although they have a superficial smoothness, the closer detail is much more varied. Crevices cleave the surface at irregular intervals, some shallow, others plunging into subterranean gloom. Between them, the face of the rock may be scratched and pitted, or curved and fluted into a myriad of undulating ridges and hollows.

Even the names of these features have a stony quality. The surface slabs are called 'clints', the clefts, most of which are only a few centimetres wide, 'grykes', with drainage runnels scooped like miniature valleys to link the two. Toying with the sound of the words, I step out and up across the ringing flats.

A party of goats clatters ahead, and I marvel at the strangeness of the noise. For my feet and theirs are being supported by the solidified remains of an old sea, which was old even before dinosaurs roamed the earth. Some 350 million years ago, shallow, tropical waters bathed this part of the planet. The life forms in the ancient sea were simple, such as the corals which grew in luxuriant reefs in its warm, clear waters, and the molluscs which burrowed in the mud of the sea floor or swam in its blue lagoons.

When they died, the external trappings of these creatures – shells and coral tubes – blended with the ooze on the sea bed. For countless coral and shellfish generations – for some 80 million years, perhaps – the gentle, lime-rich rain of life-support structures and sediments continued. Squashed down by the weight of water, with coral cavities gradually filled by a cement of calcite, then pressed and moulded by aeons of earth movements, the soft floor became hard rock.

This limestone of the Carboniferous period covers more of Britain than any other rock formation, and is the geological platform for the entire central plain of Ireland. Further deposits from the Jurassic and Chalk times take up variations on the limey theme further south and east in England, showing on geological maps like broad tide marks from much later seas.

There are obvious and often spectacular outcrops of Carboniferous limestone on the surface in widely scattered upland areas of England and Wales. These are 'karst' lands (named after a distinctive limestone area in Slovenia), where the working of water, wind and ice has fashioned deep gorges, distinctive surface mouldings and amazing underground caverns in the stone. Huge beds of this Carboniferous material are one of the dominant rock types in the Pennines, for example, with other notable chunks of limestone-flaunting country along part of the Welsh Marches, in South Wales and in the cave-rich Mendips of Somerset. In Ireland, by contrast, the great limestone sheets on the plain are tucked beneath blanketing drifts of glacial material from fairly recent times, and in Scotland, precious little breaks the surface.

But what happens undercover can be as spectacular as the overground scene in karst country, where drainage is largely a subterranean affair. Streams carrying acidic water, such as those spilling down to the Burren from neighbouring shales, can eat away at vertical cracks to form 'swallow holes', which carry them deep below ground. Once there, the water can slowly gouge and dissolve labyrinths of passages as it heads downhill, sometimes pushing its entire course for many kilometres onward to the sea at these hidden depths.

The working of water on underground rock can carve caves of monumental proportions. On the eastern slopes of Ingleborough, for example, a modest stream called Fell Beck tumbles down a vertical shaft. When it hits the rock more than 100 metres below, it splashes on the floor of Britain's largest underground chamber – a space big enough to hold a cathedral. For cavers and potholers, it's small wonder that limestone is the motherlode of adventure.

As befits a place which can have something of the look of grey Gorgonzola at the surface, the Burren is full of wonderful cave systems and passageways below ground. But here, as in some other parts of Ireland, the hidden plumbing system also works a little water magic up top.

I look down to the water of some small lakes below the hill, azure blue and clear as the

Opposite: A limestone pavement set amid grassland at Mullaghmore, The Burren, in County Clare.

sea which spawned the stone beneath. There is something mirage-like about these glinting waters, cupped in plains of dryness. Before summer is out, they will have vanished, for these are turloughs – ephemeral lakes in ice-scooped hollows which are fed, not by streams or springs, but by the groundwater in the rock beneath them. As this rises and falls according to the rains, so the turloughs swell and drain. Only one turlough is claimed for Britain – at Carmel Woods in Dyfed. So the phenomenon is an essentially Irish accord – conjured by a rare blend of geology, place and Atlantic weather.

Limestone pavements themselves are also precious few, despite the widely visible legacy of the Carboniferous sea. The reasons for this are not fully understood, for there are still several ideas about quite how limestone pavements took their present form.

The basics of the surface shapes and patterns are probably straightforward enough. When glaciers scraped some limestone flatlands clean of soil and plants during the last ice age, they left the rock open to weathering. Weak carbonic acid from rainfall could then have worked to widen the grykes and mould the clints, plucking limestone off in solution from the sunlit surface, perhaps to be added, drip by drip, to stalagmites or stalactites in the perpetual darkness of a cave far below.

Alternatively, the stone-eating water could have come from nearby peatlands, or areas of more acidic rock, or from the rotting vegetation of former plant cover, with etchings of erosion only being revealed when soil was washed away. This could certainly be true of the Burren, where clearance of woodland from Neolithic times would have started the process of baring the stone there to western Ireland's copious rains. There is even a recent idea that the clint tops once capped beds of sediment in the old sea floor and were covered by a thin layer of organic ash, which then chemically hardened their surface. If some of these processes played a more significant part in one region than another, this could explain some of the variety in the surviving pavements.

As if the remarkable history and shaping of these places – both known and theorized – is not source of interest enough, the plant life heaps on more riches. Most of the orchids in Britain and Ireland are lime lovers, so a limestone pavement in high summer can be a garden of delights for people, like me, who seldom fail to be captivated by the varied petal shapes, patterns and colours – from subtlest cream to hottest pinks – of these splendid, long-lived plants.

The Burren is blessed with Ireland's finest concentration of orchids, with at least 22 of the country's 27 species growing here. Bee and fly orchids with their insect-duping mimicry, tiny frog orchids half-hidden in grass, sweetly scented fragrant orchids and rare helleborines, are just some of the names to tempt the fancy here.

Another part of the secret for plant variety on the Burren and other pavements lies in the grykes. The shallower of these crevices can make humid havens for greenery. Ferns seem to revel in the conditions, with hart's tongue and hard shield ferns, several kinds of polypodys and spleenworts among the typical colonists. Some of the pavements east of Morecambe Bay are the British stronghold of the rigid buckler fern. And in Irish pavements, the rusty-backed fern, another rarity, is well established.

Some flowering plants also cope well with gryke life, where conditions can mimic the shady dampness of a woodland floor. This link shows clearly in the mix of crevice-dwelling flowers, such as herb robert, dog's mercury, lily of the valley and wood sage. Trees and shrubs – often wind-pruned or turned into wild bonsais by sheep or goats – add to the sense of woodland sliced and compressed in some pavement clefts. Small hazels and ash trees, junipers and blackthorns (including special ground-hugging forms in the Burren), may sprout miniature canopies only centimetres higher than the flowers which share their soil.

In other parts of the pavements, especially at fringes on the lower slopes of hills or on terraces below cliffs, taller trees can grow to form hazel, yew or ash woods of more familiar size. Even here, the ground can offer visual treats such as a pastel blue haze of bluebells, a host of primroses, the wine-coloured blooms of the dark red helleborine orchid, or the slender stems of angular solomon's seal, its white flowers hanging like waxy bells above yellow-green mosses.

But in early summer on the Burren, before the full array of orchids and other blooms is completely on song, two plants steal the show. One – the mountain avens – is a dwarf shrub typical of northern tundra. The other – spring gentian – is a flower more characteristic of alpine meadows.

Raised only slightly above ground level, millions of mountain avens flowers, each a rosette of eight white petals radiating from a core of golden-yellow stamens, seem abundant as oversized daisies as I walk. They sprout from grykes, cling to rock faces and sprawl across terraces, the flowerheads' beauty accentuated by a backcloth of tiny, dark green leaves.

In grassier places, spring gentians punctuate the turf like jets of blue flame. Their ancestors probably arrived on the Burren and the nearby Aran Islands from the south, long after the last ice sheets had gone. But the mountain avens has a longer lineage here and on the sugar limestone of Upper Teesdale (another treasure house of arctic-alpine flowers), for it is superbly kitted-out to cope with extreme conditions of winter cold and summer heat.

Its flowers look delicate, its plumed seeds ephemeral, but this belies the plant's intrinsic hardiness. The evergreen leaves are thick to store food through the winter and coated in wax and hairs to cut down moisture loss and conserve heat. Silvery leaf undersides can be angled upwards to reflect excess sun glare, or petals cupped to warm up stamens and give a free energy boost to pollinating insects.

Mountain avens is so characteristic of some tundra-like conditions that records of its pollen in sediments have been used to piece together a picture of climatic shifts, from cold to warmer and back again, towards the end of the last ice age. It figures in the Burren's pollen charts for the last 10,000 years – an indication of the harshness of the conditions here, but

Opposite: This limestone pavement, known as clints and grykes, is in the East Barrows National Nature Reserve in Lancashire.

also a sign that this place has been a refuge for it, not only before the glaciers melted, but also when other plants took over much of the ground elsewhere. Here, it can compete and thrive.

Crouching, I touch a mountain avens rooted in a crack on the Burren pavement. Its stem, twisted like a brown reptile writhing over the grey rock, is thick as my wrist. I marvel at its persistence here, where it may have weathered a century or more. One hundred such lives could bridge the divide to when the last glaciers were on the run.

Many more human generations have been lived-out in this part of County Clare since then and many have made their mark. From the cooking places of the earliest hunters, through wedge-shaped tombs built by Neolithic settlers and Bronze Age inhabitants, past Celtic ring forts and Cistercian abbey ruins to the field boundaries of the modern farmers on hillsides and valleys, human history is traced in stone over the Burren. As with the rock beneath, ancient and recent are juxtaposed. One sweep of the eye can move from Stone Age to Dark Age to present and back again. It's a dizzying combination, scarcely touched by contemporary archaeology.

For the people who still live here, winter has a special significance in the Burren uplands. Reversing the traditional, but now largely defunct, pattern of stock movement in counties with a Celtic connection, this is the time when the Burren farmers shift their beasts to the high ground. In summer, the livestock (feral goats excepted) stay near the houses in the lowlands.

It's a system of husbandry which makes good sense, and which has been followed here since ancient times. For the Burren's hillsides keep fairly dry underfoot in winter, are warmed a little by the limestone's heat-storage capacity and provide a bite of grass. Summer, by contrast, can bake the upland pavement surface to a scorching, waterless desert.

This traditional, wise use of unusual resources is in stark contrast to the rampant exploitation which has been typical of our dealings with other limestone pavements. Symbolic of this interaction is the scene in all too many places in the north of England, where the stone has been ripped apart – smashed, grabbed and taken off for quick sale after an illegal raid. Gaps bereft of surface rock and flowers, their hastily shaped geometry jarring with

the curves and tracery of natural forms, are the legacy of this selfishness.

Human pressure on the pavements has been building since Victorian times, stimulated by demand for unusual stones to add shape to rockeries or give sculptural quality to municipal flower beds. At first, chunks of pavement were removed by prising them loose with a crowbar before carting them off for sale. Later, the use of tractors and powered diggers allowed much greater amounts of stone to be extracted, causing much more extensive damage to the remaining pavement. Take a stroll along the promenades of Blackpool, Lytham St Anne's or Southport and you can see where some of it went.

In one notorious plundering, 1,000 tonnes of clints were hacked from Ingleborough to make an exhibit at the 1951 Festival of Britain. But the upshot of many decades of rock removal is that precious little pavement has survived intact. In Britain, where the total area only amounts to 2,500 hectares, a mere 75 hectares – 3 per cent – remains undamaged. Sold as 'water-worn' or 'Westmorland' stone, such rock can still fetch as much as £100 per tonne in garden centres.

Some of the trade in these last fragments is legal, for although all limestone pavements are listed as worthy of priority conservation action within the European Union, and theoretically have protection under EU and national laws, loopholes remain which allow more quarrying. In Britain, 'Limestone Pavement Orders', designed to safeguard surviving pavements, cannot override existing planning permission for rock removal.

The only way that a local authority could theoretically stop the rot would be to pay massive compensation for lost income to the quarrier – but this has never been a realistic option. So old planning decisions, made before the true conservation value and scarcity of limestone pavements was known, continue to take their toll. Coupled with illegal stone

Bloody cranesbill in the limestone pavement in clints and grykes in the Burren, Eire.

Opposite Left: Limestone pavement at Arnside near Silverdale — a designated Area of Outstanding Natural Beauty — being destroyed for use as rockery stone.

Opposite Right: Visitors swarm over the limestone pavement at Malham Cove in the Yorkshire Dales National Park.

removal, where diggers work under cover of trees or darkness, the history of these ancient places might appear to be rapidly drawing to a close.

But even as the clock seems poised to tick to midnight, people are rallying to help these special limestone lands. Damage already wrought cannot be undone, but at least the remnants could be cherished. In Britain, a Limestone Pavement Action Group has formed, backed by the Wildlife Trusts and other voluntary organisations, and supported by prominent gardeners. This is seeking better governmental protection for pavements and is encouraging people to avoid using water-worn limestone in rockeries. Alternative ornamentation is easy to make from sand, cement and coir compost, and much cheaper than buying chips from the old block.

In Ireland, it seems fitting that campaigning has focused on the Burren. In the early 1990s, plans for a multi-million pound tourist centre at Mullaghmore, in the finest part of the Burren pavements, were put forward by the Irish Office of Public Works and received financial backing from the European Commission. Construction began, but was halted when a local action group, working in alliance with other Irish and UK conservation organizations, took legal action against the European Commission for failing to comply with its own environmental policies through funding the centre. Broad cuts in the pavement at Mullaghmore, coated in slick asphalt for car and coach parking, show where the move to a quick-fix Burren 'experience' has, for now, stopped short.

The most eloquent statement of the current mood of protest against past and proposed exploitation of limestone pavements has come, not in words alone, but in melody and song, composed by Irish musicians and blended in a recording to raise funds for the Burren campaigners. In this, performers from the locally popular to the internationally famous give individual expression to their sense of this special place. The sounds of wind, stone and blackbird song and the ebb and flow of a low-register whistle playing 'The May Morning Dew' begin and end the compilation.

On a May evening, I descend from the hill of Mullaghmore, head reeling with images of flowers and rocks. Down on lower ground, I dip my warm limbs in a turlough, savouring the coolness of water, thinking of ancient seas. A breeze rattles old reed stems and breathes ripples on the water, and a blackbird sings in an apple tree. A gentle splendour blossoms from the fertile rock.

Right: The remains of a limestone pavement being used as a rockery at Lytham St. Anne's in Lancashire.

Opposite: An extensive limestone pavement with tourloughs at the Burren in County Clare.

travels of their ancestors, from Neolithic times onwards, as I stand in an electrically-lit sheep shed, and discuss the fortunes of the latest generation of lambs with my relatives.

As if the range of downland breeds was not variety enough, a description of a Wessex sheep fair by Thomas Hardy in *Far from the Madding Crowd* suggests that sheep owners – or would-be sellers – boosted their sales pitch last century by a liberal application of fleece dyes:

> 'Thus in a slow procession, they entered the opening to which the roads tended,
> multitude after multitude, horned and hornless – blue flocks and red flocks, buff
> flocks and brown flocks, even green and salmon-tinted flocks, according to the fancy
> of the colourist and the custom of the farm.'

Traditionally, downland pastures were used by allowing the sheep to graze freely by day, then bringing them down for 'folding' by night on low-lying fields. So the sheep effectively shifted energy – through their production of mutton, wool and dung – from the high ground to the low. Such a drain on resources, as well as the mechanical action of the grazing itself, could have further helped to shape the downland vegetation. This is formed by plants which can cope with stresses of life on ground where growth-boosters, such as nitrogen, potassium and phosphorous, are in short supply, and where competition for scarce resources in the dense sward is intense.

The kinds of plants which best withstand the twin challenges of food shortage and frequent chomping, are perennials. These include both potentially fast growers, which can shift gear and chug along at a more sedate rate, and naturally slow-growing species which demand little food to survive. The sheep's fescue grass, named for its superabundance in downland turf, is a classic example of the latter, undemanding group.

Overlaid on that basic plan of campaign for plant life on the chalk are many variations. Fourteen different major types of calcareous grassland community have been identified by the National Vegetation Classification in Britain, with a host of smaller variations within them to add distinctive local colour. A major split in these communities is between a northern group and a southern group, separated by a line which runs from Durham, through Derbyshire, to the Mendips, and skirts the southern seaboard of Wales. South of that line – which roughly separates wetter uplands from drier areas – chalk-seeking or 'calcicole' species, including several at the northern limits of their European range, give a really distinctive character to the swards.

Even a partial roll-call of widespread chalkland plants is a tempting wish-list for those who hanker after botanical pleasure: quaking grass with its shivering flowerheads, owner of a host of local names; dwarf thistles – crimson petalled and devillishly prickled; salad burnet, whose bruised leaves smell of cucumber, and have a piquant flavour; common rock-rose, whose stamens recoil at a finger's touch; traveller's joy, adding a sprawling anarchy of growth to hedges and trees stems; basil, marjoram and thyme, giving a scent redolent of the Mediterranean to the warm turf underfoot – aromatherapy for the soul. Sprinkle in orchids, such as fragrant, bee and burnt-tip, and localized rarities – Chiltern gentian, wild candytuft, pasque flower and squinancywort – and the list is heady indeed.

Mosses, liverworts, and lichens further spice the plant mix, which in places can top 50 different species in a square metre of turf. Many kinds of invertebrates live in these grass-lands, which can support an abundance of snails and sustain many kinds of bees, wasps, crickets, grasshoppers and beetles. But it is the ants and butterflies which often grab attention on the downlands – the former through the hummocks raised on the turf by meadow ants, the latter for the sheer splendour of their appearance.

For calcareous grasslands, especially in southern England, are prime territory for that most beguiling group of butterflies – the blues. With underwings often freckled with dark spots and trimmed with orange, and the upper wings of the males (except for the small blue) dominated by blue, these are insects to tickle the visual fancy. The chalk-hill and common blues seem crayoned in pastel; the large blue (now reintroduced) packs a punch with size; but the Adonis blue, whose name honours the mortal paramour of Aphrodite, goddess of love, is a shimmering cobalt flake of heaven brought to earth.

There would have been many places in southern England which were blessed by such colourful summer fliers many centuries ago. Grasslands on the downs probably reached their maximum spread in the late Middle Ages, after a gradual increase in numbers of people and sheep following the ravages of the Black Death. Parliamentary enclosures nibbled at the edges and large areas were ploughed to grow corn during the Napoleonic Wars in the late eighteenth and early nineteenth centuries. But the downlands remained the power-house of lowland British sheep production until the early decades of this century, with their roving flocks of motley breeds keeping swards in fine trim for many choice flowers and insects which relish the conditions in warm, southern grasslands.

'Cultivation Orders', introduced in 1940 as a means of compelling farmers in certain areas to increase food production, changed all that, promoting widespread ploughing and conversion of downland turf to arable. By the 1950s, enthusiasm for grazing sheep on nutrient-poor 'unimproved' pastures was on the wane, so that downlands which had been spared the ploughshare in previous decades now began to fuzz over with taller grasses, such as tor grass and upright brome, and sprout more bushes and seedling trees.

At precisely this delicate point in the downland balancing act between grassland and woodland, the scales were tipped even more strongly in favour of trees. When the myxo-matosis virus was unleashed among British rabbits in 1953 and eventually dispatched, with its vile suppurations, at least 99 per cent of the entire rabbit population, there were many who viewed the epidemic – loathsome though its symptoms might be for individual animals – as a boon, releasing crops and young trees from costly nibblings by massed legions of bunnies.

Opposite: Shepherds' cottages on the South Downs in Sussex.

The downside – both literally and metaphorically – only later became apparent. For the previously abundant rabbits (descendants of animals brought to Britain by the Normans, and relative latecomers as free-ranging grazers away from the confines of closely tended warrens), had been performing a sterling service for the downland swards. As sheep numbers dwindled, the rabbits had been doing (or chewing) their bit to keep the old pastures open. With their virtual extinction in the years before myxomatosis-resistant strains appeared, the decline of chalky grasslands accelerated still faster.

Rapid losers in this process of human-speeded succession from one type of dominant vegetation cover to another were the blue butterflies. The British representatives of this attractive coterie are a finicky lot. Their fate is usually linked to a single food plant – such as horseshoe vetch, kidney vetch or wild thyme, which their larvae eat – and with particular ants.

These can help to protect caterpillars above ground (in return for a reward of sugary secretion), and shelter them in their nests, or bury them underground when the time comes for the caterpillar to attempt its marvellous metamorphosis from earth-bound crawler to delicate skydancer. Short grasslands on the downs can keep things sweet for the blues – helping food plants and meadow ants to thrive, and holding temperatures cosy at ground level for the warmth-loving butterfly larvae – for some of which southern Britain is the northern extreme of the world range of their kind.

As rabbits tumbled, grasses grew and the blues were chilled out. The Adonis, already rare, fell even further from grace, and along with chalk-hill blues (and silver-spotted skip-

What was once glorious Sussex downland has been turned into this featureless cereal prairie.

pers), disappeared from many areas. Only one rare butterfly, the Lulworth skipper, seemed to benefit briefly from longer grass and expanded a little from its few Dorset enclaves.

Worse was to come, through the application of fertilizers to some downland swards. General scarcity of nutrients, such as nitrogen and phosphorus, is one of the keys to floral variety on the downs, for if the slim pickings of plant boosters are coupled with grazing, this effectively stops fast-growing grasses from shading out less pushy sun lovers. In this sense, on chalky as well as on limestone soils, a little of what plants fancy can do wonders for their diversity. But since stiff shots of nitrogen, phosphorus and potassium have been the agro-chemical order of the era for grassland fertilizers, even a single hit of such a potent spray could floor the flowers, and let tougher grass triumph.

Things began to shift a little again in the 1980s and 1990s, when rabbits, helped by the rapid evolution of their twentieth-century plague into a plethora of less deadly forms, began to bounce back. Increased EEC subsidies on mutton and beef also began to make it profitable – in some cases for the first time this century – to put sheep and cattle back on the chalky grazings.

Conservation bodies, too, were getting heavily involved in livestock husbandry, as the Nature Conservancy Council (now English Nature), began to use grazing as a tool to reinstate open grassland in places which had shifted to bush and tree-dominated ground in earlier decades, and the Wildlife Trusts established flocks and employed shepherds and shepherdesses to tend them. But surviving chunks of flower- and insect-rich downland are mostly small indeed in comparison to the spread in former centuries.

Such shrinkage and fragmentation have sorry implications for some downland creatures, such as butterflies which find it hard to migrate over inhospitable ground and whose isolated colonies become more vulnerable to extinction. Yet this is not so different from the tales told elsewhere in this book about so many other kinds of wildlife-rich ground. What set the downlands apart for a while in the early 1990s was the sheer strength of response when yet more destruction was mooted, this time with the full backing and might of the state.

The first legal moves to re-route the M3 motorway through the middle of Twyford Down near Winchester were made in 1984. This date is significant, because it was later used by the UK government to argue that it meant that there was no requirement for a 'Environmental Impact Assessment' of the roadworks to be produced, as would have been necessary under the conditions of a later EC Directive. This effectively barred the public from proper consultation about the scheme.

When the road-building juggernaut began to roll towards its Twyford target in the early 1990s, this lack of accountability began to bear bitter fruit. Twyford is a much-designated Down, with two sites of Special Scientific Interest, two ancient monuments and its posi-

Right: Beulah sheep grazing in the Devil's Kneading Trough at Wye and Crundale in the Downs National Nature Reserve in Kent.

tion in an Area of Outstanding Natural Beauty as accolades which reflect its landscape, archaeological and ecological importance.

But such designations were reduced to the status of bureau-babble when the time drew near for the bulldozers to roll. For it quickly became clear that the UK government was deaf to all but the demands of its transport department. It was even willing to push aside the stipulations of its own Wildlife and Countryside Act and risk confrontation with international conservation directives by sanctioning the destruction of part of Twyford Down.

In the end, it was people, not statute, which came between the bulldozers and the downland turf. For a short while, they held back the forces which were to destroy an ancient village site, trackways and field systems, and which would cut a 130-metre-wide swathe through orchid- and butterfly-rich pastures, including England's largest colony of chalk-hill blues. Helped by Winchester residents, members of the recently gathered Dongas Tribe – a small band whose name was derived from the most threatened part of Twyford – lived on the doomed land for nine months until the bulldozers and security men moved in.

On the first day of attempted road construction, the tribespeople and locals stopped the bulldozers in their tracks. On the next day, the security men and contractors returned, backed-up by some 50 police. They rapidly set about arresting protesters and began felling and burning trees and bushes.

When the bulldozers sliced the first turf from the ancient sward, it was a scalping of huge importance. It signified the destruction of more than just this one piece of downland, cherished and even venerated though that was. For the power of the state had been used to crush its own flimsily-framed conservation measures, and to quash those who stood in support of this ancient landscape and its wildlife.

As the white gash of the motorway cutting was ripped into the Dongas Down, it cut to the heart of Twyford, then deeper. For if the chalk is part of the very stuff that helps to define the wider British nation, then this was one hell of a wound, symbolizing a divide between state and people, between natural qualities and unfettered forces of development.

Now it is plain to see – a monstrous totem whose spirit is utterly at odds with the earthy symbols of earlier peoples, cut as gigantic celebrations of fertility and local identity in other downland slopes. For this represents a wholly different spirit; one whose white scar bares the darker side of a dominant tribe's soul on the embattled downs.

Right: A Duke of Burgundy Fritillary butterfly.

Opposite: Whitebeams growing on downland at Ivinghoe Beacon in the Chiltern Hills, Hertfordshire.

The sad sight of an ancient meadow that has been ploughed, this example in Langdale in the Lake District.

of the horse-drawn mowing machine last century, this would be done by teams of scythe-wielding mowers walking line-abreast through the meadow. Others came behind to turn and spread the hay with rakes and forks – a process which could help to disperse the seeds of meadow flowers and grasses. Next, the hay would be pushed into windrows, then propped up to dry further in haycocks if the weather still held good. Once the grass felt light and dry and was properly 'cured' it would be carted off for storage in haystack or hayloft.

The building of haycocks and haystacks gave yet more scope for variation in the look of meadows. But the meadow plants themselves also added regional flavour, a little of which can still be tasted in the surviving unimproved grasslands. Fritillary meadows are essentially a feature of floodplain ground in southern and eastern England, and quintessentially of the upper Thames and its tributaries. Green-winged orchids can also be prominent in damp meadows in the East Midlands, with cowslips in better-drained meadows, and meadow saxifrage and meadow cranesbill on drier grasslands further east.

To the west, where old grasslands have survived marginally better in Worcestershire and Avon than in many other English and Welsh counties, the meadow saffron – an autumn

flowering crocus which emerges after the usual time of haymaking – can still raise its smooth, lilac-pink-suffused flowers straight from the turf, naked of leaves. But it is a far cry from Victorian times, when Edward Hulme wrote of the meadow saffron that: 'we have in some places seen quite a purple flush of colour on the meadows from the presence of count-less blossoms, but it is a sad blot on the pasturage to eye of the owner, for it takes the place of much that might be edible.' Further west again, some Welsh hay meadows still harbour creamy spikes of greater butterfly orchid, or the dark blue, claw-like flowers of wood bitter vetch.

A distinctive northern mix takes prominence in the meadows of northern England, espe-cially in the Pennine Dales, including some plants which are more familiar as woodland dwellers further south. Wood cranesbill, globe flower and melancholy thistle are some of the specialities of places like Swaledale and Teesdale. Sheep's fescue, cocksfoot, quaking grass, meadow foxtail, false brome and, of course, sweet vernal grass, are some of the herbage names to tickle the fancy on the meadows of these limestone soils, plus blue moor grass on the pastures where the exquisite little bird's-eye primrose may also wink from the turf.

The variations from meadow to meadow and pasture to pasture can be enormous here, adding an element of surprise to their exploration. But the field barns, built to store hay over winter, are a unifying strand. These box-like, two-storey stone buildings, many now abandoned, which give shelter for animals on the ground floor and have a hayloft above, stand proud of the network of drystone walls as one of the most distinctive landscape features of the Dales.

Despite a reduction in the variety of grasses and flowering plants in many of these meadows, as here too, the use of fertilizers and the convenience of silage making has spread, at least some of the botanical richness has been kept, thanks to the designation of the Pennine Dales Environmentally Sensitive Area, or 'ESA'. This was one of the first ESAs established in the UK, in the wake of the Agriculture Act in 1986.

There are now more than 40 such areas, as different as the valley of the chalk-bedded Test in the far south and the windswept hill grazings of Shetland in the north. But in all of them, there is a recognition that traditional farming methods have a crucial role to play in maintaining the special wildlife, landscape, and archaeological interest of an area. This is coupled with an understanding that to continue these long-established methods can involve a financial cost to farmers, who might otherwise use quicker, cheaper, or higher yielding contemporary techniques. So subsidies are paid to farmers who agree to follow certain ways of working, or carry out specific jobs – such as the rebuilding and maintenance of stone field dykes – which will protect some of the features for which a particular area has become valued.

The beauty of this system is that, although it involves some bureaucracy in the form of

Opposite: An upland farm in North Wales where the hay meadows have been converted to silage pasture.

five-year agreements between individual farmers and the agricultural departments who administer the scheme, this is based on plans appropriate to a particular farm, and drawn up because the farmer has chosen, not been coerced, to enter the scheme. So giving extra cash for agreed work can also make economic sense. Crucially, it can help to maintain, not only the natural heritage features which make an area attractive to people who live far beyond it, but also the livelihoods of residents who continue to work in and shape that area.

Because of the mix of methods followed, both on farms which join the ESA scheme, and those which pursue other paths, the blend of farmscapes is not fossilized, like some kind of agricultural theme park, but can alter and evolve. The drawback is that this kind of arrangement is not applied much more widely, since many farms, communities and the wildlife connected with them elsewhere could all benefit from such an approach.

Within the Pennine Dales ESA, the main thrust of environmental subsidy goes to keeping the distinctive hay meadows abloom, as well as helping to conserve stone walls, field barns and small woodlands. To maintain the meadows, farmers in the ESA agree to keep stock out of them for at least seven weeks before the first cut of hay or silage, for example. They also do not cut before a particular date, calculated to be the best one within a particular dale for helping plants to thrive, as well as for the farmer to gather a useful harvest of fodder.

In Dentdale and Deepdale, for example, the earliest cutting date in ESA meadows is 1st July. For Wharfedale, Langstrathdale and Waldendale it is a week later; while the first environmentally subsidized hay is taken from the higher fields of Swaledale and Arkengarth Dale, Teesdale, Weardale and Rookhope in the middle of the month.

A further spin-off to this pattern is that it is a boon to the many wading birds, such as snipe, redshank and curlews, which nest in the meadows, and which can rear their broods in the long grass before the mower appears. An earlier cut, and some of their chicks could literally get the chop. This principle of old grassland husbandry to benefit both flowers and birds (and the people whose work, founded on the practices of many generations, has boosted them), reaches its zenith in Britain and Ireland in other ESAs, on the 'machair' grasslands of Scotland's Hebrides.

Machair is a Gaelic word, applied to a plain of coastal ground, inland from an Atlantic shore and seaward of the peaty hinterland, where lime-rich sand, composed of the fragments of countless millions of shells, has been blown by the prevailing westerly winds. This provides a seedbed of great fertility. It has enormous importance, both locally to agriculture, and internationally, because of its store of plants and birds. Machair also occurs in Ireland – where coastal developments, including the construction of golf courses, have much depleted it in recent years. But it is in Scotland that it achieves its global peak, especially on the Inner Hebrides of Tiree and Coll, and the outer islands from the Sound of Harris, south through the Uists to Barra and Mingulay.

Here, the concentration of breeding dunlin is as high as anywhere in Europe, with many other waders, including oystercatchers and lapwing in the shorter turf, and redshank and snipe in the longer grass, nesting in numbers which are now astonishing in comparison to mainland meadows and pastures. Thanks to these birds, it is the sound, as well as the sight and smell of the machair which is so beguiling.

Moderate grazing, often in a meadow pattern where stock are excluded from some areas during the peak summer growth period, but where the dung from sheep and cattle adds further fertility to swards in autumn and winter, is one key to the botanical richness of the machair. Different lengths of sward, some grazed as pastures, are one of the secrets of the waders' success there.

The contrast between machair areas within one island can be as great as the variety of Pennine meadows, while the changes from island to island are even more striking. On one, wild carrot, meadow cranesbill and meadow rue may predominate in late summer. On another, bloody cranesbill arrests the eye with the intensity of its purply-red flowers, set against a background of pale shell sand, where kidney vetch and bird's-food trefoil add shades of yellow and orange.

Elsewhere, such as on the pastures of Tiree, the sheer extent of a single flower can be breathtaking. An entire field blanketed in daisies, buttercups, or white clover, is a source of wonder for modern eyes wearied by the monotony of uniform greenswards on the mainland. Finally, in wetter meadows, the pink tatters of ragged robin, spikes of heath spotted and northern marsh orchids and the glossy yellows of buttercups and spearworts, mingled with the greens and reds of fescues, plantains and grasses, echoes the mixture in the rain-soaked meadows of western Ireland, where such an exuberance of growth and colour can still be enjoyed in small fields of Atlantic-fringed counties, such as Galway.

The flowery meadows of Ireland and Scotland are further linked through the fate of the corncrake – a relative of the moorhen – which is more closely associated with hayfields in the summer than any other European breeding bird. This hefting to a particular type of farmland has been its undoing, for the agricultural changes of the last century have pushed the corncrake to the very brink of extinction.

Now listed as globally endangered, the corncrake has declined throughout Europe. Once, its rasping, repetitive call, given incessantly and in the middle of the night by males in their summer territories, was a prominent feature of the farmland scene in many places. It was variously regarded either as noise pollution, or as a harbinger of the season, (depending, perhaps, on the proximity of the writer's or singer's own dwelling place to a calling corncrake): 'But when cold winter is awa', and summer's pierced the sky, we'll welcome back the corncrake, that bird of rural joy', run the last lines of a nineteenth-century song of love and courtship among the summer meadows, which uses the corncrake as a repeating motive in its verses.

The timing of the corncrake's decline in different counties of Britain and Ireland was closely linked with the local spread of hay cutting by machine from the last century

Opposite: An old crofter's plough on the machair, South Uist in Scotland.

onwards. This was possibly because of actual deaths of adults and chicks, trapped in the centre of fields as cutting moved from the edges inwards. The bird's fall to the verge of extinction came through the loss of haymeadows themselves, from the earlier mowing dates associated with silage, and from the drainage and 'tidying up' of wet patches – thick with reeds and yellow flag irises – which can give cover to corncrakes early in the season before meadow grasses have grown high.

One of the few hotspots for this summer-visiting skulker is in the flood meadows or 'callows' of the River Shannon (one of Western Europe's last major rivers still allowed to follow its natural course, unfettered by major drainage schemes) in Ireland, where many of the Republic's less than 200 males still call. The other is the machair of the Hebridean crofting townships, where all but a handful of the fewer than 600 craking males remaining in Britain place their summer calling cards.

Years of research work by the RSPB into the corncrake's precise breeding requirements have been followed by that organization's purchase of farmland on the island of Coll, specifically to manage meadows and damp cover for the benefit of corncrakes. Coupled with this science and conventional reserve-based work, have been innovative partnership schemes, both in Britain and Ireland. These include the cooperation between the Scottish Crofters' Union and the RSPB in Scotland, where, helped by funding from the European Union, and from the UK government through the ESA schemes, farmers and conservation groups have been working to give a lifeline to this beleaguered bird.

The corncrake has vanished from England, Wales, Northern Ireland and most of Scotland, and its future is still by no means secure, but there have been encouraging local increases elsewhere as a result of the new partnerships. Its health seems to depend on the kind of flower-rich farmland where heavy input of human effort is matched by a light hand on the agrochemical bottle, and where there is a sensitivity to the traditions of husbandry which have been shaped by the environmental conditions of a particular place. That is an appealing blend, as attractive in its way as the meadows themselves.

Perhaps the corncrake and the crofts of the far west, rather than representing a nostalgic echo of wildlife which has been lost elsewhere, and a farming pattern confined to the fringe, give a pointer to how things could be arranged much more widely. They outline a state of rural affairs where the diversity of both human and wildlife communities still matters. So the modes of operation of such farming seem central, not peripheral, to contemporary concerns. Keep calling, midnight crakers, for at last more people are hearing the messages from the meadows.

An oystercatcher surrounded by buttercups in Hebridean machair.

LET'S BOOM AGAIN

t's a bravura bathtime performance. From a froth of foam, I pluck an empty plastic bottle, put it to my lips and blow, gently and steadily. A deep, resonating note, breathy and complex with undertones, issues from the garish purple container. My son, aged three, makes an appreciative comment about the 'funny noise'. My daughter, aged one, reaches out to grasp the bottle, then experiments with its voice-changing properties before dropping it and grabbing a yellow duck.

The sound is fun to hear for a few seconds – something out of the ordinary to add interest to the nightly routine. Just a game, but one which reminds me uncannily of a sound I heard a long time ago, in a reedbed hundreds of kilometres away from here.

I pause, wondering if – distant mimicry apart – the children will ever have the chance to hear such a sound as natural music, issuing from deep within the screening plants of a large wetland. The odds seem stacked against it, for the voice I recollect is that of the bittern – a bird whose preferred breeding places in Britain and Ireland have changed in ways not much to its liking in recent times, and whose fortunes are currently at a low ebb. For now, concentrating on the plastic ducks seems a cheerier option.

Later, I recall another scene which seems to catch a different aspect of the allure of the wetlands – more common, yet not commonplace. In a reed-fringed lake in the early morning, with a thin mist still hanging like breath in the cool air, a swan glides out over the calm surface. Its reflection is distorted by ripples as it swims, but its solid form is a splendid confection of white plumage. It sees another swan, half hidden in the tall stems, and moves rapidly towards it, arching its wings in a slow flowering of carefully poised threat, like a giant waterlily on the move.

Then it blows a raspberry. The aggressive noise is enough to frighten the intruder, which hurries away to open water, then takes off, feet splashing, wings flailing. Once in flight, the sound of air whistling through its feathers is electrifying.

Sound and silence, action and pauses, familiarity and unpredictability: wetlands seem to hold all these things. Perhaps it is because their combination of open water and close-clumped vegetation almost inevitably blends the obvious with a sense of the hidden, or with a partial knowledge of things heard, but yet unseen. Perhaps it is because water and greenery are such primal parts of enjoyment of wild places for most people.

'Lake water lapping with low sounds by the shore,' runs part of Yeats' alliterative description of an island which might yet be found in some calm, freshwater settings, but which also symbolizes a state of mind. Many of us could still value an Innisfree, and it is a fair bet that Ireland may yet harbour such a retreat, for it has both water and lakes in abundance – a bonus from its plentiful rains.

Some Irish lakes are huge, thousands small. In Northern Ireland alone, there are more than 1,100 of them. Most don't top ten hectares, but Lough Neagh, fed by six major rivers which pour into it from several points of the compass, and spread out across nearly 400 square kilometres, is massive – one of the largest freshwater lakes in Western Europe.

In winter, Lough Neagh hosts a wildfowl population to match the scale of its waters. A count of nearly 10,000 goldeneye, made here on a March day in 1987, was one of the highest ever recorded in Europe; the 1,700 scaup which winter here are the continent's biggest inland concentration; and the flocks of tufted duck and pochard can outnumber those anywhere else in Britain and Ireland.

Elsewhere in Ireland, apart from the attractions of the numerous lakes with turbid waters, marl lakes formed over beds of chalk or limestone beguile with their clarity. With limestone widespread beneath much of Ireland's soil, marl lakes are commoner here than in most parts of Europe, and can sustain varied wildfowl – from coots to whooper swans – which can graze on the deep-anchored vegetation, such as stoneworts, which may thrive in them.

In Britain, there is a pronounced upland/lowland divide in the character of bodies of freshwater. Upland ones tend to be deep, with stony shores and food-starved waters. The abundance and variety of different forms of life – from microscopic creatures to plants, insects and birds – is much less in these than it is in the shallower, lowland waters over softer beds of mud or clay.

This division is particularly obvious in Scotland. Many Scottish hill lochs seem almost bare of fringing plants, and silent, save for the sound of the wind. But the shallow lowland lochs, their waters thick with a soup of foodstuffs, their edges lush with emergent plants, hold an obvious living throng.

Swallows and martins chasing gnats and other swarming insects above the surface; ripples and bubbles from fish rising; gangs of duck busy in the shallows; coots and dabchicks making high-pitched comments; dragonflies hawking the fringes; reed buntings casting throwaway songlines to the breeze – these are all familiar sights and sounds of lowland waters, both in Scotland and further south. In Wales it could be a valley floor llyn, in England a flatland lake, mere, or broad, but the principle holds true: still waters run deep; busy waters spread shallow.

The biggest difference between countries is that, with the exception of the meres in Breckland, and on the plains of Cheshire, Shropshire and Staffordshire, virtually all the lakes in lowland England are artificial. Their origins lie mainly in flooded mineral work-

Opposite: Upper Lough Erne in the Croom Estate, Fermanagh in Northern Ireland.

ings, reservoirs of different kinds, ornamental creations and flooded peat diggings – a far cry from the generally natural beginnings of large-scale open waters in other parts of Britain and Ireland.

Luckily, wetland wildlife seems to pay scant regard to the niceties of waterbody roots. Artificial lakes in the Midlands, for example, have as much variety in their birdlife as the natural meres. Taking the broader range of wetlands into account, from seasonally flooded grazing marshes to plant-rich fens, England's finest, without exception, owe their status as havens for water dwellers to human action. This includes work carried out in the past and work which continues today. For, like so many other places now valued for their distinctive wildlife, the suitability of these wetlands for a wide range of different creatures and plants diminishes without continuing intervention. Here, it is sometimes a case of 'spare the reed and spoil the bed'.

The tallest native grass in Britain and Ireland, the common reed is of vital importance to some of the most prized wetland wildlife, including very rare birds, such as bittern, bearded reedling and Cetti's warbler. All of these prefer reedbeds of more than 20 hectares in extent as their breeding place.

But reedbeds of that size are very scarce. Only 33 were noted in the whole of England and Wales during an RSPB survey carried out in 1979 and 1980, from a total count of a little over 100. Scotland and Ireland have few large reedbeds and many small ones, but these don't host as many different species as the big 33 in the other countries.

Within England and Wales, chunky reedbeds are both rare and patchily distributed. Most are near coasts. About half the big Welsh beds are in Anglesey, and in England, the major concentration is in East Anglia. Here, an area bounded by the coast from Lowestoft to Sea Palling on its seaward side, and stopping short of Norwich to landward, holds reeds aplenty. This is a flatland threaded by many channels and punctuated by dozens of shallow lakes – the so-called 'Broads'.

Hickling, Barton and Martham, near Potter Heigham in the north; Wroxham, Cockshoot and Ranworth south of Bure; Filby, Ormesby and Rollesby, then Oulton in by Lowestoft. These are some of the names to roll on the tongue, rich sounding as Norfolk and Suffolk dialects, redolent of a mix of Scandinavian and Anglo-Saxon influences which shaped the villages here, and of the unusual landscape which surrounds them.

Most of the Broads owe their existence to former peat workings. More than 25 million cubic metres of fen peat was extracted from Broadland in the Middle Ages. This activity was probably at its peak in the thirteenth century, boosted by the commercial acumen of local monasteries, which acquired the rights to dig and dry peat in many parishes (each broad is in a different parish), and put squads of peasants to work for their benefit. Floods and rising sea level ended the mega-scale diggings, although small-scale extraction continued in some places until last century.

Having created the Broads, people could reap a useful harvest from their natural productivity – as they also did in the Cambridgeshire Fens – harvesting reeds and saw sedge for thatching, mowing hay from the marsh ground to use as fodder and bedding, and grazing livestock on the drier margins. This was a life-saver for the area's fenland character. For in the natural course of things, reedbeds and shallow areas of open water in lush lowlands are usually a stage on the way to the development of something else.

Regular reed cutting is one way to halt the progression before the next moves to dry ground and trees. The harvesting stops litter from piling up, keeps the plants vigorous and closely packed and is often associated with controlled flooding of the beds to a shallow depth in summer. All this helps to keep the competitors at bay, and a fen in good and soggy fettle. As a bonus, digging and dredging of channels to provide access to beds for removal of cut stems creates openings within the dense stands. These are narrow enough to be largely screened from disturbance, but there is space enough for fish and eels to use them all year, and for otters, herons and others – including bitterns – to follow.

Hunting pressure and wetland drainage pushed the bittern to extinction as a breeding bird in Ireland in the middle of last century. It was extinct in Britain by 1865, but recolonized Norfolk by 1911, later spreading to Suffolk, Lancashire, and Humberside, and eventually to Kent and Wales.

The comeback was precarious, however, peaking at perhaps 80 boomers in the 1950s.

Friesian cows grazing on Caerlaverock Marshes in the Wildfowl and Wetlands Trust Nature Reserve in Dumfries.

Opposite: A reed marsh at Leighton Moss RSPB Reserve in Silverdale, Lancashire.

Only male bitterns boom, issuing their *basso profundo* notes as a challenge to rivals and a come-on for females. Given the chance (which is now a slim one in most parts of Europe), males also mate with more than one female, so the conversion of calling males to potential broods is not straightforward.

Nuptial complexities apart, the message from the reedbeds through nearly half a century has been clear: the bass has bombed. Currently, there are fewer than twenty boomers in possible British breeding sites, mostly in Norfolk and Suffolk. An occasional bird pipes-in at an Irish reedbed, but no breeding has been known there since the demise of the bitterns of Munster, Connault and Ulster last century.

Interpreting this message has been more difficult, requiring careful study of bittern lifestyle to fathom it. Deciphered, the accepted text now runs that loss of suitable hunting areas, especially watercourses in and beside big reedbeds, as well as shrinkage and transformation of the beds themselves, has made all but a few places uninhabitable for bitterns.

Insult may also have been added to injury by increasing pollution of once-clean waters,

Thatching with Norfolk reed.

particularly due to enrichment from domestic run-off and agrochemicals. Such a cocktail has been a sickener in Broadland, turning clear waters cloudy, fuelling clogging growths of algae, accelerating the infill of open water, killing plants, fish, eels and insects, and generally squeezing down the variety of life, for which the area was reknowned, to a poorer, simpler mix.

Add to this the twentieth-century ultra-nasties, such as organochlorine pesticides, PCBs and mercury – all of which can be carried to wetlands and build up to high levels in living tissues. Complete the brew with a large dose of pleasure boat traffic, creating wash, spilling diesel and adding noise and disturbance to previously tranquil scenes. The question then becomes, not one of why many creatures have declined, but how they cope, against the odds, in an environment so utterly different from that which persisted for centuries from the Middle Ages onwards.

A recurring theme bursts to the surface again. For what came about through human action on the large fenlands, and then was compromised by the withdrawal of traditional activities, and the substitution of fierce new pressures, could once again be restored by careful intervention.

Such work is already underway, both in the Broads, and in many other wetlands. At Strumpshaw Broad, the RSPB has pumped out sediment, chopped willow and alder carr, cleared out dykes, expanded open water and started reed cutting again. Reed cutting has also been revived at the organization's Leighton Moss Reserve in Lancashire, and at its famous Minsmere Reserve in Suffolk. The results are dramatic. Marsh harriers, Savi's and Cetti's warblers have moved in to breed at Strumpshaw, where bitterns now visit and amphibians and reptiles have been boosted. Otters, deer, duck and bitterns are benefiting at Leighton Moss, and at Minsmere, bitterns have bounced back from a low ebb of one boomer in 1991 to several successful nests by the middle of the decade.

On the Broads, although some reed and sedge is still cut on a commercial basis for thatching, there is now no profit to be made from the digging of fen peat. But fresh cuttings are being created, initially through cooperative work by English Nature and the Broads Authority, to make new areas of open water and fen and so-called 'turf-ponds'. These can give living space to stoneworts, pondweed, bladderworts, duckweeds and rare plants, such as lesser water plantain and bog pimpernel.

There is still a huge amount which could be done, for the projects mentioned here are small-scale in comparison to the overall extent of Broadland, and the complexity of what has been lost. But it is a bold start, offering new possibilities in a changed landscape.

There could also be many other opportunities, both familiar and novel, for positive change in other types of wetlands. For the huge, government-backed, post-1940s enthusiasm for land drainage, kindled by a desire for greater output and efficiency in production of farmed food, and fuelled by liberal applications of grant aid, has subsided. There is now

Opposite: Recreational development of the Norfolk Broads as seen on the River Bure at Horning.

an increasing acceptance of the importance of wetlands as part of wider systems, with a role to play in flood prevention, maintenance of underground water reserves or 'aquifers', and pollution control.

Growing demands for crop irrigation, especially in eastern Britain, have sucked some aquifers dry in areas which have also been subjected to heavy drainage and land 'reclamation' works in the past. Restoration of surface wetlands could ease the underground crisis, adding to the overall regional water store and trickle-feeding replenishment down to the aquifers. Such a natural linkage has never been lost at the margins of some of the grand and meandering Irish rivers, where 'callows' – or seasonally flooded meadows – work winter transformation of land to water, thronged with wildfowl. This then sustains a bright and lively community of wildlife through spring and summer, after the floods subside.

The callows by the mighty Shannon, between Athlone and Portumna, are the very finest of such places, with other splendid callows by the Suck, the Little Brosna, and the Blackwater. These host ducks, geese and swans by the thousands in winter, while golden plovers probe the edges. In spring, they welcome wigeon and black-tailed godwits on stop-over visits during journeys to Iceland, then give space in their rushy, silt-gorged flats to breeding lapwings, redshank and snipe.

If the bittern is in some ways the primadonna of the marshes, apparently able to play only to the most select of audiences in the choicest of venues, the snipe is its complete opposite. Able to find breeding space in tiny patches of rushes, content with a little mud to feed in, and drawing attention to its precise position with squeaky calls when it lifts into zig-zag flight, the snipe is at home and obvious in a host of damp, marshy and boggy places. The farmlands of western Ireland and the western edges of Scotland, spared the worst excesses of drainage and agricultural intensification elsewhere, are custom-made for it, with their damp pastures and rushy tussocks.

The Irish callows reflect a continuing part of the traditional wetland scene, but newly created reedbeds are at the cutting edge of change, assuming an increasingly popular role as clean-up champions. It has been known for a long time that contaminated water can be made wholesome by passage through a wetland. This could come about for a number of reasons, such as filtration, chemical change and biological action. Whatever the physical and chemical background to the purification, reeds seem to be particularly good at it.

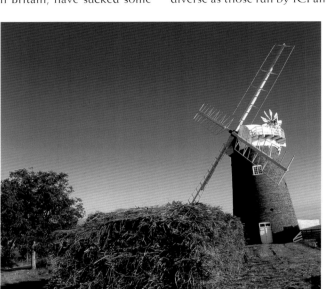

Sedge grows close to the windmill at Horsey Mere on the Norfolk Broads.

During the last decade, there has been a great increase in the creation of reedbeds planted specifically to tackle different water-borne pollutants. Yorkshire and Severn Trent water authorities now use reedbeds to treat domestic effluent, and factories – including ones as diverse as those run by ICI and The Body Shop – have begun to install reedbeds to remove industrial waste. These have mainly been created and designed with an eye to their pollution control function. But there is also scope, without compromising that ability, to fine-tune the shape and inner details of new beds to make them more useful for wildlife.

That's the principle behind the construction of a reedbed filter system at the Slimbridge Centre, run by the Wildfowl and Wetlands Trust. This uses a mixture of features, including a lagoon, cascades and overland flows, associated with the reeds, to give a way of treating effluent and expanding feeding, breeding and resting areas for wetland birds and other wildlife.

In comparison to the reedbed story, both in long-established fens where the reeds and their denizens are being helped by bold schemes, and in the recently established beds, where extra value can be given to plant-powered pollution control, the situation for lowland wet grasslands may seem altogether shakier. The Irish callows retain their wet splendour, though some would see it dried out. But in Britain, names like Somerset Levels, Ouse and Nene Washes, Derwent Ings, Amberley Wildbrooks and the Pevensey Levels turn thoughts as much to a catalogue of drainage and shrinkage in recent decades, as to the simple richness of their silt-boosted grazings.

Once, more than a million hectares of lowland wet grassland thrived in England and Wales, with stores of food and water replenished by winter flooding. Their swards were kept useful for wildfowl and waders and open for a large range of plants by low-pressure agricultural use, through grazing or mowing. Without this, as in reedbeds, bushes and trees could move in and change the open grassland to closed woodland cover.

Now, only about a sixth of the former spread remains, reduced by a shift of gear to intensive farming, which led to conversion of the old grasslands to arable fields, or to other radical changes of vegetation through higher stocking levels and widespread silage production. Coupled with many schemes to convert wet grasslands to heavier-duty use, came

Opposite: A grey heron stalks amongst a reed marsh.

Visitors enjoying a nature trail at Ranworth Broad Nature Reserve in Norfolk.

drainage works, designed to reduce or prevent the old cycle of flooding, and to rapidly dry the saturated soils, which had now been targetted as prime sites for greater food production.

Of the lowland wet grasslands that survive in England, less than 10 per cent of their area is now ranked as of high value to wildlife, sheltering the abundance and variety which gave such places their natural richness in the past. Yet, here also, a key to that richness came both from the regular patterns of human use which maintained the grazings and meadows, and in many places, also from the historical efforts which moulded their landscapes in the first place.

The Somerset Levels – a great swathe of country below sea level, held in the basin of a former lagoon, and overlooked by the Mendips and the Blackdowns – came into being this way. Every part of the land here has been won from water and marsh. Transformed by a network of seawalls, ditches of different kinds, pumps and sluices, and criss-crossed by a tracery of drove routes and green lanes, this ground now supports some of the finest dairy herds in England.

Other herds – of wintering Bewick's and resident mute swans – add to the fame of the Levels, as do visiting and breeding waders, a dazzling array of dragonflies and damselflies, the large and leggy raft spider, and a range of plants which includes the rare and tiny root-less duckweed – no bigger than a grain of sand. The ground available for such species diminished as the use of high-efficiency diesel and electric pumps expanded.

Early moves to protect surviving wildlife havens in the Levels, by designation of 'Sites of Special Scientific Interest', met hostility from local farmers, inflamed by a reaction against heavy-handed bureaucracy and by a desire to continue meeting the agricultural goals of one government department, in the face of conflicting demands for nature conservation from another. In the worst of the inglorious confrontations generated by such official inconsistency, effigies of conservation agency staff were hung from gibbets on the Levels.

Those dark days have gone, thanks to a partial shift of government policies (prompted by food surpluses in Europe) towards greater integration of agricultural and environmental aims, and to the willingness of farmers to participate in an Environmentally Sensitive Area scheme, which now covers most of the Levels. Yet, despite the great sums of money spent in the ESA, and the goodwill of most of the people who care for the Levels, numbers of certain creatures, such as wading birds, have continued to decline there.

Part of the problem seems to come from the sheer extent of drainage interconnections, meaning that a big push for continuing dryness in one part can have an undesirable, dessicating effect elsewhere. A way forward now being explored is to sever some drainage links. This could allow blocks of land to be flooded in winter and be maintained through traditional means as moist pasture – good for livestock, plants and birds – despite drainage elsewhere. It is a problem not confined to the Levels, and one which is also leading people to think big and bold about new possibilities. Essentially, the larger the area included in schemes to conserve wet grassland, the more confident you can be about securing its future squelchiness.

Acquiring and maintaining such land will be costly. But with shifted targets for agriculture, an appreciation of the natural contribution of floodplains to water storage and flood defence, and a willingness by government agencies, voluntary conservation bodies, farmers and other land users to work together, large-scale restoration is possible.

Reedbed rejuvenation and creation projects are paying rich dividends for wildlife and people in fens both old and new. If it is being done for the benefit of the rare and strange, such as the bittern, could the time not also be ripe to use water, that great leveller, to do likewise for the potentially commonplace snipe?

Opposite: Britain's only turlough, at Carmel Woods in Dyfed.

THE WILD WET BLANKETS

Where the moorlands of Sutherland dip to meet the plains of Caithness, the largest expanse of blanket bog in Europe stretches away to the eastern horizon. Bog mosses dominate the vegetation for more than 4,000 square kilometres here, covering old red sandstone rocks and their echoes of ancient deserts with a cold compress of deep peat. Locals call this place 'the Flows'.

When I first saw the Flows, through the windows of a train travelling northwards to Thurso, the immensity of the bogland was awesome. It was like looking out on a mossy ocean, with few surface features to help judgement of distance. This lack of reference points to judge the scale of things was intriguing – a challenge to my previous sense of natural perspectives in my home country – and I determined to come back again on foot some day, when there would be time to explore the sodden flatlands.

When I next saw the Flows, an alien fuzz of conifers sprouted from trenches gouged in the living skin of the bogs. I knew something of the damage this would do to the wildlife here – changing a productive refuge for scarce birds, plants and insects into something which would be useless for these creatures. But with little more than a glance, I could also see what had been done. In the very heart of the Flows, the young trees had wrecked the old sense of vastness. The new plantations gave easy reference points. They made it possible to estimate distances, and to realise that even this great plain was contained within fairly tight bounds.

They made me feel quite big again in relation to the landscape, but there was something deeply disturbing about this altered sense of proportion. For I remembered how it had been just a few years earlier, when there had been an inkling of a different scale of things.

The new order seemed precarious, but it was a sign of the times. Peatlands, from the smallest lowland bogs to the great blanket bogs of the uplands, are almost everywhere under siege from forestry, peat extraction and agricultural development pressures.

Many have already vanished. In Ireland, the vast Bog of Allen, which once stretched from the outskirts of Dublin to the Shannon River, has been destroyed to provide a few years' supply of fuel for Irish power stations. In Lancashire, the mosslands which were once scattered throughout the county have all but gone – drained for agriculture and reduced to two surviving fragments. Other lowland bogs are suffering death by a million growbags as their peat is milled down and carted off to be sold to gardeners.

In the uplands and along Ireland's Atlantic fringe, conifer plantations are claiming more and more territory from the blanket bogs. Yet some of the remaining bogs are still ranked as the finest of their kind in the world, for parts of these islands have the perfect climate for bog mosses.

In cool, wet areas in the north and west of Britain and in western Ireland, where the rain from Atlantic westerlies falls on 160 days or more each year, conditions are ideal for the formation of peatbogs. Rain spawned the largest mires in these places, where more water falls from the sky than evaporates, and rain feeds their slow growth. Elsewhere, peatlands form in places where drainage is poor, perhaps because of a clay soil, and which are flooded by watercourses and groundwater in addition to rainfall.

In waterlogged conditions, there is little oxygen to fuel the bacteria and fungi which usually help to break down plant material in the soil, so the decomposition of plant remains slows to a crawl. As layers of dead plants accumulate, the water around them becomes more acidic, darkening the debris as it presses together to form peat. The type of peat produced depends on the source and richness of the water which feeds the mire.

Fen peat accumulates from the lush growth of sedges, rushes and flowering plants in places where the water is rich in plant foods. This can happen in river plains, as it did on a grand scale in the silted plains of the East Anglian fenland and the marshes of the Somerset Levels, both of which have been almost completely drained and reclaimed for agriculture. In Norfolk, peat diggers removed large quantities of fen peat for fuel in medieval times. Their flooded workings now form the Norfolk Broads (see 'Let's Boom Again').

Rainwater is deficient in minerals, so conditions in the bogs which form in heavy rainfall areas are often quite acidic, making life at the surface impossible for any plants not able to cope with sourness. Sphagnum mosses, which make up the great bulk of the plant material in acid bogs, thrive in these pickle-jar conditions. They even add to the acidity by swopping nutrient salts for hydrogen ions in the water which seeps through the bog.

There are 30 different species of sphagnum in Britain and Ireland, each suited to life in particular sites, such as hummock tops or pool margins. Dead sphagnum is the main ingredient of the dark brown to black moss peat which forms in the upland blanket bogs and in raised bogs and which provides a superior fuel to fen peat. The small mosses shape the largest boglands and give them colour, carpeting the surface in greens, yellows, oranges, pinks and reds and often changing from subtle buff to deepest claret in the merest finger width of space.

In northern and western areas, where conditions are wet enough for peat to form on level ground, great tracts of sphagnum cloak whole landscapes. 'Blanket bog' is an apt description for this mossy mantle, which is restricted to these areas and which has moulded both the appearance of the land surface and the lives of the people there. The main expanses of

Opposite: Deer grass in a regenerating raised bog in Roudsea Moss National Nature Reserve, Cumbria.

Atlantic blanket bog are in western Ireland, the Welsh uplands, the Pennines, the Cheviots, the southern Scottish uplands and the Highlands and Islands.

Globally, blanket bog is rare, being found only in places such as western Norway and Tierra del Fuego where there is the necessary mix of cool, humid conditions and gentle slopes. About one-seventh of the world's total area of such bog, estimated at some 10 million hectares, is found in Britain and Ireland. Some of the finest examples anywhere on the planet are in the Flows of northern Scotland and the bogs of Mayo and Connemara.

Raised bogs – immense domes of peat overtopping hollows which once held lake vege-tation – are the other great sphagnum creations for which these islands are famous. Like blanket bogs, they rely on rainwater for the nourishment of their growing surface layer. But they generally form in lowland areas, where bog mosses have taken their acid hold of peat-lands formed under sweeter conditions in the still-water swamps of lakes and other wet hollows. As the central part of such a mire swells with peat, it steadily rises relative to the edge, where moss growth is held in check by conditions beyond the margins, and so forms the classic dome of a raised bog.

In gently sloping valleys, where the flow of water along a central stream is quite slug-gish, bogs can develop which are not wholly dependent on rainfall and climate, but are more a product of the local terrain and the plant nutrients available there. Because of this, these valley bogs are widespread in both upland and lowland areas. They vary greatly from place to place, forming moss peat in nutrient-poor conditions, where sphagnum can thrive, and fen peat in richer, sedge-dominated conditions, such as the bogs of the New Forest.

The plants of raised bogs and blanket bogs do not vary so much from place to place as those in valley bogs – the harshness of the mineral-starved environment narrows the range of species which can live there. But they have a simple beauty, drawn from strong colours and bold contrasts. Aside from its sphagnum coat of many colours, a typical stretch of summer bogland may be white with cotton grass, saffron with bog asphodel, green and purple with heath and heather and flushed pink and red with the drooping flowers of cran-berry. A pale froth of bogbean flowers in the dark pools and the aromatic scent of bog myrtle add to the variety.

Segregation of different plants according to their individual preferences for particular conditions of moisture, shading and temperature adds to the texture and patterning of the bog surfaces when seen from close by. But the most dramatic patterns are caused by the interplay of standing surface water and the plants which surround it. The full splendour of the patterned blanket bogs is revealed from above. From a hill or from an aircraft, their lattices of dark pools – some tiny and clustered, some large and solitary – and the ridges and hummocks which stipple the moss ground in between, make the lumpen bogs look delicate, like living tissue.

The features which pattern the bog surfaces also add to their value for wildlife. Pools harbour water beetles – fodder for frogs, toads and newts – and provide good hunting space for dragonflies such as the black darter. Ducks such as teal may breed there, their young

thriving on the midges and other small insects which can make life difficult for humans who venture across the bogs in summer. In the north of Scotland, common scoter and both red- and black-throated divers nest beside some of the lochans, where otters dive for fish and wildcats pad the shores.

Golden plover and dunlin are the most charac-teristic wading birds of upland bogs. The mournful whistles of a golden plover, the bird often invisible behind a hummock or shrouded in mist and rain, have a soft melancholy which captures something of the spirit of these places, as the fuller drumming of snipe does for the lowland bogs. In the Flows, trilling greenshank, which are only thinly scat-tered outside this area, add shivering cascades of sound to the summer scene.

The spread of the bog mosses which mould these wildlife havens first began in Scotland and the Pennines around 7,000 years ago, and was pushed into overdrive for 2,000 years by the heavy rainfall in the warm, wet Atlantic period. On places such as the island of Lewis, peat has been produced in abundance from then onwards, so that even the standing stones at Callanish – raised there by Neolithic skygazers – were largely hidden by peat when Sir James Mathieson exca-vated that beautiful, cruciform monument several thousand years later, in 1857. Most of the blanket bogs in Ireland and central Wales date from early Bronze Age times, about 4,000 years ago, whereas some on parts of Dartmoor and Exmoor appeared later.

Timbers of ancient trees, which died at times when local conditions became too wet for their kind, are a widespread feature of the bogs in

Ireland and Scotland. But the peat archive stretches wider than simply recording the trees of past eras. The pollen grains which settled on the bogs and became trapped there, which drifted in their billions from bog plants and from trees and herbs far removed from the mires, give a record of past climatic changes and shifts in vegetation over many plant eras.

Above: Chat Moss in Lancashire is being destroyed for the manufacture of horticultural peat.

Right: Seen here drying, this peat has been hand cut in the traditional manner.

Cores of peat removed from the three raised bogs of Tregaron in Wales are just one of the sources of this time-locked pollen information, which paleobotanists have used extensively to build up a picture of long-vanished plant communities. But every bog has its own store of pollen history, with local variations on the national themes of advancing and retreating vegetation types. Such information takes on a new significance in the current period of global warming, where records from the past could give some idea of the possible patterns of changes which could still lie ahead.

Peat can also hold fragments of human history in airless time-lock. Ancient timber causeways on the Somerset Levels; prehistoric boundaries of the Ceide field systems in Co. Mayo; hordes of butter in bogs elsewhere in Ireland; farming implements and weapons of war; and even the preserved bodies of people – such as the famous 'Pete Marsh', the princely sacrificial victim from Iron Age Cheshire, now housed in the British Museum – have all been uncovered, enriching understanding of long-vanished cultures. As the bogs are destroyed, the archive is smashed into smaller and smaller pieces. It can never be recreated.

The reek of peat smoke from Irish cottages and Scottish crofts still gives a distinctive tang to the air in our western and northern fringes. Its blue wisps may seem like a romantic haze to some visitors, but peatlands have been both a blessing and a curse for the people who have lived beside them during the last few thousand years. During recorded history, the bogs have been variously seen as wastelands, fit only for drainage, reseeding and reclamation for agriculture, and as valuable sources of fuel and other material for sale or subsistence.

In the blanket boglands, peat was often the only accessible or affordable fuel. Sustained habitation in places which did not have a ready supply of peat was often impossible, or, at best, precarious and difficult. Dried peat makes a clean, slow-burning fuel, but harvesting, stacking and drying it for the fire can be laborious and time-consuming.

But times are changing, even for the small peat harvesters. New machinery can allow one person on a tractor to complete in a single day the digging work that once took a fortnight. The temptation to cut more than a family needs, to sell to others, and to reclaim more bogland for agriculture, is too great for many owners of these small machines to resist.

Larger machines are helping to destroy the few remaining lowland bogs, scouring their surfaces for horticultural peat and scooping them up for fuel. Most of the raised bogs in England and Wales have already disappeared and the bogs of lowland Scotland are increasingly being used for commercial cutting. A study which compared the areas of boglands shown on maps made in 1860 with the situation in 1978 found that only 4 per cent of the former area of raised bogs in lowland England and Wales still remained. Drainage for agriculture and forestry had claimed the other 96 per cent in little more than a century.

There has been further attrition since then. In the mid-1990s, the Scottish Wildlife Trust's Raised Bog Conservation Project team (now sadly disbanded), working in partnership with Scottish Natural Heritage, said that the pace and scale of degradation of that country's raised bogs was leading to their total extinction as a functioning ecosystem. Of the other lowland British bogs which still survive, the majority have been damaged by draining, burning and cutting.

Ideally, such places should ooze water and defy easy access, but that is seldom the case these days. To walk dry-shod over raised bogs, as I have done many times in places designated as nature reserves and reckoned to be amongst the finest surviving mires of their kind in Britain, gives a ready demonstration of just how far removed such areas now are from the natural systems which spawned them and which are precariously close to annihilation in these islands.

In Ireland, peatlands originally covered more than 17 per cent of the land surface – a higher proportion than in any other European country except Finland. Hand-cutting of peat for fuel has been carried out in a sustainable manner in Ireland since time immemorial. Large-scale, mechanised turf cutting has only gone on since the 1940s, yet it now threatens to eradicate the raised bogs of the Irish Midlands.

The Irish Peat Development Authority, Bord na Mona, was founded in 1946 to extract peat on an industrial scale to provide jobs, money and energy. With an annual production of around 10 million tonnes, Eire is now second only to the Soviet Union in the world peat extraction league: (about 90 million tonnes of peat are excavated in total each year). It is also the only country outside the Soviet Union which generates electricity from peat-fired power stations.

Bord na Mona uses large machines, weird looking as lunar landing vehicles, to scoop peat from the Midland bogs. These either skim the top off the bog, leaving a loose layer of powder to dry for use as milled peat, fuel briquettes and horticultural moss peat, or they cut the raw peat into sods. The country's major power stations consume millions of tonnes of Irish peat each year, but Eire is also the world's leading exporter of moss peat, which is principally sold for use in British gardens. By the mid-1990s, less than one tenth of the original area of the raised bogs remained undamaged by peat extraction, drainage and burning.

Blanket bogs are also being fragmented, changed and destroyed. Industrial pollution and earlier cuttings have taken their toll of some, such as the South Pennines peatlands, but the biggest changes in the blanket bogs have been caused by drainage and planting for forestry. Plantations of exotic conifers are claiming more territory each year, both in upland Britain and in western Ireland.

Nowhere has this been more apparent, and more bitterly contested, than in the Flow Country. The relative inaccessibility of the Flows meant that the value of the area was not widely recognised until the early 1980s, when it was realised that the sheer extent of these great mosslands, and the tundra-like bird community there, made the Flows possibly the most important blanket bog area on the planet.

But the forestry ploughs were already making their mark. In what the UK government's conservation agency described at that time as the most massive loss of important wildlife habitat in Britain since 1945, one private forestry company, Fountain Forestry, planted lodgepole pine and sitka spruce on about 16,000 hectares of pristine bogland during the

Above: A traditional peat cutter gathering peat dug from Chat Moss in Lancashire

Left: Some alternative mulches to peat on display in a garden centre.

1980s. The mauling of the Flows was funded by rich investors, who in turn were heavily encouraged by the Exchequer through tax concessions for new plantings. These tax breaks have since been removed, almost certainly in response to the massive criticism generated by the controversy in the Flows.

In 1988, the Secretary of State for Scotland finally admitted the international importance of the area and said that about half the unafforested bogland could be given some statutory protection under an expanded network of Sites of Special Scientific Interest. The following year, the UK Government announced plans to dismember the Nature Conservancy Council, by splitting it into separate agencies for England, Wales and Scotland – a move which has since weakened the influence of those agencies and which many conservationists interpreted as revenge for the old Council's stand over the Flow Country. The delicate beauties of the sphagnum lands are no match, it appears, for the schemes of politicians.

Despite such machinations, both in the bogs themselves and in the corridors of power, there are still some glimmers of hope for the future of at least some of the remaining mosslands. In Eire, the Government committed itself several years ago to acquiring 10,000 hectares of raised bogs and 40,000 hectares of blanket bogs for conservation. It is still nowhere near achieving this target, but there is a feisty and tireless national advocate for bog conservation – The Irish Peatland Conservation Council – to keep jogging its memory and prod international consciences over the fate of the Irish bogs.

Thanks to the work of IPCC and others, several Irish bogs have been purchased in order to cherish them as wildlife havens. Clara, Scragh and Bealacoon are three such bogs, bought with money from sources as diverse as fund-raising in the Netherlands (where people now lament the near-complete loss of their own bogs, destroyed for fuel long ago), hefty grant aid from the European Union and donations from thousands of IPCC supporters. Educational and artistic ventures, developed by IPCC and bogland devotees elsewhere, and well-conceived new visitor centres, such as that beside the Ceide Fields, have also helped

to scotch the myth of bogs as lifeless wastelands and have done a great deal to foster appreciation of their soggy splendours during the last decade.

Aiming to further boost such changed attitudes to bogs, the Northern Ireland Department of Environment has opened 'Peatlands Park', which combines a country park, nature reserve and mini railway. In England, the purchase of Fenn's and Whixall Mosses in Shropshire as a nature reserve (by English Nature) was a major event in the early 1990s. Conversely, a deal between English Nature and peat extractors to conserve only part of Thorne Moors (a place where the so-called 'National Nature Reserve' sits like a doomed and dessicating alien landform amid a desert of cut-over bog) pleased few other than the bureaucrats and businessmen who engineered it.

In the mid-1990s, the RSPB's purchase of the huge Forsinard Estate, in the heart of the Flows, was followed by a large-scale partnership between that organization, Scottish Natural Heritage and Caithness and Sutherland Enterprise, backed by a grant from the European Union's LIFE programme. The upshot of this high-flown-sounding alliance has been an exciting project to help local crofters and others to work in conserving the northern blanket bogs, increase the provision of information about them and support green tourism ventures based on the environmental assets of the area.

Elsewhere, techniques pioneered by the

Conifer plantations encroaching on typical Flow Country in Caithness.

Scottish Wildlife Trust's raised bog team have helped to reinstate some wetness to large areas which were previously dying of thirst, and provide methods of working which could be applied much more widely. So in just a few years, many different strands of activities in both Britain and Ireland have added to the economic worth of the bogs for local human communities, while helping to ensure that their wildlife communities have a more secure future.

Another encouraging development in the 1990s has been the great increase in the use of alternatives to peat in horticulture and gardening. This was prompted by pressure from

Opposite: Bog cotton fringes a raised bog pool at Malham Tarn in the Yorkshire Dales National Park.

a 'Peatlands Consortium' of ten conservation groups, concerned by the continuing destruction of raised bogs to provide bedding, mulching and seeding media for plants. Such uses
of peat have burgeoned only since the 1930s, before which gardeners used their own
compost formulas, usually based on loam.

Use of peat substitutes, such as coir – which can provide material as good or better than
peat for horticultural purposes – has been boosted by the consortium and by support from
influential people such as the late Geoff Hamilton on the BBC's 'Gardener's World'. The
majority of local and regional councils in Britain and major organisations such as the
National Trust have now gone peat free, with no detriment to the vegetation in their care,
but with potential benefit for the bogs which are still being stripped of their ancient moss
cover.

Yet several million cubic metres of peat are still used by both professional and amateur
plant growers in Britain and Ireland each year. This is despite the availability of alternatives
and the enormous scope for household and municipal compost to be used (as is required
by law in Switzerland) for planting schemes.

More people than ever before are now aware of the wildlife riches of the British and Irish
bogs. But the living bogs, where mosses thrive and sundews glisten, are getting fewer and
drier by the year. There is a strange irony in the thought that compost from the decayed
tidyings of well-tended gardens could help to protect these wild places, where the peat is
swelled by the lack of decay. It just needs a different sense of perspective.

Right: A curlew nesting amongst bog cotton in the Fenn's and Whixall Moss National Nature Reserve, Shropshire.

Opposite: Blanket bog surrounding a lochan on the John Muir Trust's Sandwood Estate in Sutherland.

THE SHIFTING MARGINS

Landscape and seascape are pared down to cool simplicity here. The pebble strand, formed from billions of rounded stones that slip underfoot, curves away to east and west and merges with the December fog. It slopes sharply behind, blocking the landward view, and dips to meet the North Sea surge.

A thin line of whiteness smiles where sea and beach merge, hissing, in a brief and tumbling embrace of water, stone and air. I look beyond it, peering into gloom, and scan the sea surface. Sea ducks, divers or dolphins could be out there at this season – or something stranger.

I recollect how the carcase of a huge sperm whale washed ashore not far from here some winters ago – like a creature from another dimension, cast up as monstrous flotsam on the land, to be gradually worn to nothing by waves and scavenging gulls. But today, the slate is blank of other signs of life. I walk on grey stones, by a grey sea, under a grey sky – a lone

Roosting curlew, knot and oystercatcher on the Dee estuary in North Wales.

traveller on a shifting shore, treading a narrow divide between elements, preoccupied by a wintry sense of transience.

It could be different in so many ways on so many other margins. For the coasts of Britain and Ireland are hugely varied. From the vast and breezy strands of south-west Ireland to the wave-pounded ramparts of northern Scotland, or the cosy inlets of South Wales and the West Country to the muddy flats and saltings of East Anglia and Essex, the scene is seldom constant for more than a few kilometres. Even in north-west Scotland, where glacial scour and melt has etched scores of fjord-like sea lochs into the rocky seaboard, each arm of water has a distinctive character, some broad and airy, others more constricted.

A simple division between hard and soft coast explains some of the diversity. On rocky shores, often exposed to the onslaught of gales, and pummelled by waves pushed in tall as buildings from the ocean storm track, cliff heights may be giddy and the coast can seem like a rampart deflecting sea from land. The Cliffs of Moher and Achil, breasting the Atlantic swell in Ireland; the sheer basalt faces of St Kilda, out within gannet glide of the continental shelf; the great Kame of Foula; and the crags of Clo Mor above the seething Pentland Firth – these are the coastal giants of Britain and Ireland.

But the press of elemental forces is obvious on many other rocky shores, even those whose skyward thrust is miniscule in comparison with the western and northern monsters. For erosion is a mighty sculptor of the hard fringes, working through the energy of unrelenting waves. Where a shore is exposed to open ocean, the waves that hit it can build up awesome power and volume in their landward roll, packing a punch equivalent to the weight of several bull elephants smashing onto each square metre of rock. That's on a middling day.

In the worst of weather, when gales can gust to hurricane force on the most exposed Atlantic coasts, topping more than 200 kilometres per hour before they rip wind-gauges from their mountings, the pressure is greater still. Even the toughest granites will yield to such an onslaught over millennia of storms. And the sea is quick to work on any lines of weakness in the rock, prising open fissures, undercutting cliffs, hollowing caves and blowholes, isolating pillars of more resistant rock from the softer beds that may have snuggled them for aeons, then pressing on until these too tumble, adding their shattered pieces to the debris on the sea floor and finally their substance to the sands.

Simply keeping a grip on such battered surfaces is a major problem for any plants and animals which choose to live on the hard fringe. Tough shells and fronds and a superglue

Opposite: Rising sea level has caused this coastal erosion at Holderness in Yorkshire.

approach to anchorage, coupled with shapes that can cope with the forces in all but the sea's most violent moods, are some of the keys to existence here.

The bonus of all this adaptation from a human perspective is a brilliant mix of form, texture and colour. Seen at low water on a day of spring tide, when the sea ebbs out as far as the kelp beds beneath a cliffy coast, the glistening rocks are alive with interest, their pools more vibrant and surprising than the most carefully constructed aquaria of human invention.

Exploring the intricacies of rock pools is a pleasure with obvious power to enthral many people, from toddlers upwards. For the sense of discovery – of peering into a realm of new shapes and vibrant pigments – can be irresistible. There is also something rather magical about a place which reveals part of itself for only a few hours each day, and then is cloaked by the sea again.

This daily process of covering and uncovering, linked to tides, winds and ultimately to the waxing and waning tug of the moon on the earth's magnetic field, lends a certain frisson to a walk along any coast, through the knowledge that what is now visible and touchable will soon be out of reach. On rocky coasts, this concept has extra sparkle, since some of the pools in the lowest part of the shore may only be accessible for a few hours each month. A glimpse of some of their encrusting corals, red seaweeds and tiny fish is always intriguing, and there can be added allure if some dweller from the open sea has been temporarily trapped there between tides.

One day in high summer, having crunched over barnacle-encrusted ledges and across boulders stuck with dry green weed, I came across such a creature in a cleft near the sea's edge on a Scottish island. Its body was like a small piece of lilac cloth, undulating in the water. But the astonishing aspect of this animal was the flashes of luminescence, winking and rippling over its skin like fairy lights.

Even in the glare of morning sunshine, the light show was breathtaking. In the ocean darkness, its cool fire of dancing colour must beggar description. To this day, I have not discovered the creature's name. And that, in a way, seems as it should be. For the image of that one animal now somehow encapsulates for me, through its beauty, strangeness and abiding mystery, part of the tingle of encounters with wildlife at the divide between elements.

Away from the hard-edged coasts, soft shores of sediments keep a much lower profile.

The moulding of relief here is a gentler process, sometimes born from the very sluggishness of water and particle-laden shallows. Estuaries are the archetypal coastal softies. Fed with solids, both by the twice-daily advances of the tide and by the steady transport of silt and stones down rivers which disgorge into them, they are plump and malleable.

Their oozing muds teem with life, which is big on abundance, but short on variety. Hundreds of animals of a few different kinds, from tiny *Hydrobia* snails and shrimpy *Corophium*, to lengthy bristle worms (such as the fearsome-looking ragworm) can cram into just one bucket load of estuarine mud. The most obvious signs of this abundance come, not from seeing the mud-dwellers themselves, but from other signs – such as the countless mounds of squiggly lugworm casts exposed on wet mud at low tide, when flocks of waders and wildfowl rise like living smoke against the sky.

For many of these birds, estuaries are essential stopover places on itineraries that may take them from Africa to the Arctic and back again, via Europe, in the course of a single year. Probing the ooze of a British or Irish estuary could be just what a bird like a dunlin, knot or godwit needs for refuelling before moving on. For others, such as grey plover which hold feeding territories on the mud, or geese and wigeon which graze eelgrass or saltmarsh vegetation, they can be the places which make life possible through an entire winter.

The numbers of these birds are mind-boggling. More than 2 million wildfowl and waders use the soft shores of Britain and Ireland as stopover points every autumn and winter. Over 200,000 of them could be on the Wash on just one day during that time. On the same day, Morecambe Bay, the Ribble, the inner Moray Firth, and the inner Solway could be hosting more than 100,000 birds each. Add in the tens of thousands at other coasts, such as Strangford Lough and the Wexford Slobs, the Dee, Humber and Thames estuaries, and the figures begin to blur – like a massive dunlin flock seen jinking and swirling on the horizon – at the edge of vision, beyond easy comprehension.

Heap on other statistics – that 90 per cent of the turnstones in north-west Europe spend

Above: Chemical pollution on the Cumbrian coast of the Irish Sea.

Opposite: Sea pinks, broom and scurvy grass growing on the cliffs surrounding St. Bride's Bay on the Pembrokeshire Coast.

the winter on our estuaries; that the entire Svalbard breeding population of barnacle geese winters on the Solway flats; that one quarter of all oystercatchers wintering in Britain depend on Morecambe Bay. Edge in the notion that the peak tally of birds at one place reflects only part of a rolling programme. So, since birds arrive and depart in their migration along the eastern Atlantic flyway on a daily basis, even counts in the hundreds of thousands may fall short of the actual numbers using any one stopover. The importance of the soft shores of Britain and Ireland for international bird conservation is massive and inescapable.

Yet these are places under intense pressure from people. This is nothing new. The current shape of most of our estuaries is due in large measure to human influence from at least Roman times onwards, through the raising of walls to hold back the tide and claim higher ground on the saltings for grazing and agriculture, and through dredging of channels.

But in the last hundred years, the pressure has grown more intense. In this time, Tyneside has lost virtually all its inter-tidal land, for example, while more than 90 per cent has vanished on Teesside. Part of the reduction here, and elsewhere, has come through the siting of industrial works on estuaries.

These places have been a soft touch in more ways than one. Often located at a distance from major human settlements, and with land that could look, at first glance, worthless until greened by drainage and protection from the sea, estuary edges now hold great accumulations of oil refineries and other chemical processing and production plants – the kind of factories that few people would choose to have near their own backyards.

Seen from a distance on a winter's night, when a blaze of floodlights throws huge towers, snaking pipework and vented vapours into theatrical prominence, such mega-works have a certain sci-fi allure. But consider the areas of estuary that have been taken in human hand by dockland developments such as at Felixstowe, or which could or will be swamped by tidal barrages, such as the notorious Cardiff Bay scheme, and the twinkling brightness on the reclaimed mudflats holds scant comfort for wildlife conservation.

Development of marinas and their associated buildings is reducing estuarine extent still further. Boat berths are heavily concentrated along the south and east coasts of England, with about three quarters of the total moorings in Britain sited from East Anglia, south and west along the channel coasts. Unlike marinas, estuarine moorings are not usually reckoned to need planning permission, and so can spread largely unregulated, as demand increases.

Prime sites for marinas in Britain have now all been developed, so new marinas typically need a large amount of associated work, to form breakwaters and dredge a mooring basin. Constructing properties adjacent to a new marina can be one way of offsetting these initial costs, but this makes the loss of coastal land for wildlife even more acute.

The current coastal squeeze is not restricted to the building of new structures, be they factories, docks, marinas, or exclusive dwellings. Other processes are at work which are accelerating the alteration of the soft coasts at a pace unprecedented for many thousands of years. Rising sea levels are already making their mark along large stretches of coastline in southern and south-east England. Part of this is due to Britain's long-term tilt.

During the last ice age, the huge weight of ice over most of northern Britain pressed Scotland down slightly, while southern England rose upwards. Following the ice melt, the land has very slowly settled back again, with north-west Scotland rising and south-east England sinking. The rocking motion of this readjustment is incredibly slow, and, more than 10,000 years on from its start, it still hasn't finished.

This is one reason why the soft coasts of Essex and some other parts of Eastern England are now taking a dip. The other is global warming. The most recent estimates suggest that, between now and the middle of next century, average sea level worldwide will have risen by thirty centimetres or more, as seawater expands in rising temperatures and oceans are swelled with meltwater from ice caps. To put this in context, this is roughly forty times the increase recorded during the last 100 years.

Around Britain, sea level is currently rising quickest along the Channel coast, from the Solent eastwards, at the rate of up to 8 millimetres a year. In the Thames estuary and the north Norfolk coast the rate is less, at between 2 and 5 millimetres a year. But such tiny changes are still sufficient, over fairly short periods of time, to completely innundate some flatter coastal areas.

Saltmarshes – those low-lying areas at the edge of estuaries, sheltered bays and sea lochs, criss-crossed by a fretwork of channels, and heavily used as grazing areas by wildfowl and livestock alike – are the places most at risk in southern England. They take shape very slowly, as specialized vegetation gets a grip on tide-edge silts and gradually stabilizes patches of ground. So, given sufficient time, saltmarshes could persist by moving a short distance inland as the sea swamps their former domains.

But such gentle migration is not a straightforward option in many places, for sea walls – built to protect coastal land from flooding, or to enclose higher areas of saltmarsh as grazing or building land – bar the way. So such coasts are literally being squeezed, between the rock of coastal defences and the watery place now being created by rising seas.

The damage to them is being further accelerated by the way the incoming tide swirls around in front of sea walls and scoops-up the mud that supports the saltmarsh plantlife. Due to processes such as this, more than a quarter of the saltmarsh around the Essex coast has vanished since the late 1970s.

This loss is not only a blow to wildlife, such as happens with the disappearance of little groves of glasswort, sprouting like tiny cacti from the ooze, the blotting out of the colours of sea aster and thrift, and the removal of ground where wigeon and brent geese can nibble stalks and cattle can graze the salty grasses. It is also costly in other ways. For saltmarsh, in common with many other coastal features such as beaches, buffers the land from the impact of sea.

Right: The Tees Estuary SSSI under the shadow of heavy industry in Cleveland.

Far Right: The RSPB Nature Reserve at Morecambe Bay in Lancashire.

Sewage on the tideline of a holiday beach at Blackpool in Lancashire.

A mere 6-metre-wide strip of saltmarsh can make the building of sea walls further inland easier and cheaper – halving the height needed to stop most flooding and cutting the cost of materials by a third. Without the saltmarsh, a higher, costlier wall is also more at risk of being undermined.

So taking steps to preserve such features along soft coasts makes sense from many points of view. This is why English Nature is now advocating what it calls 'managed retreat' along some coasts – arguing that it is prudent to remove or abandon some areas to the inevitable rise of the sea, while allowing sufficient space and time for features such as saltmarsh to develop on adjacent land.

This is a topsy-turvy concept in some parts of England, where generations have grown used to the idea of the present saltings as ground ripe for future reclamation. But it is a notion that would have appealed to that misunderstood monarch, King Canute – or Knut – who ruled England from 1016 until 1035, after deposing Ethelred 'the Unready'. The whole point of his apparent attempt, on one famous occasion, to turn back the tide, has been missed in many later tellings of the tale. For he was trying to demonstrate to his courtiers that only God could control the tide, not man. Nearly a thousand years later, there is an uncanny topicality about that story.

Another 'management' phrase which has also come into wide usage in recent years in a seashore context is the term 'coastal zone management' or 'CZM'. It is an expression which can sound as off-putting as many other eco-buzzphrases, but nevertheless covers some exciting moves to bring many different groups of people together to help shape future use of coasts.

The basic thrust of CZM is to promote environmentally sensitive use of coasts, and to encourage strategic planning of development and activity there. That's easily said, but it is a big idea and a huge task, potentially taking in everything from pollution control to coastal defences, dolphin watching to marine dredging, shipping movements to recreational use of beaches.

In many different places, fora have been established to help people get involved in influencing the future of their own stretch of coast. Harbour masters, pleasure boat owners, coastal farmers, tourism promoters, marine biologists, drainage engineers, planning officials, conservationists and councillors are amongst the motley crew in a typical forum. Unlikely shipmates, perhaps, but these groups are the best vehicle on offer at the moment to get coastal conservation and development unstuck from a morass of conflicting interests.

The conflicts won't disappear, but at least representatives of different points of view now have the opportunity to meet, discuss and help to influence changes in coastal use. Sceptics might brush aside these CZM groups as mere trendy talking shops, but the reality is that in some notable places, such as several major estuaries, previously bedevilled by a lack of communication between a plethora of agencies, organizations and individuals with a stake in the area, people are now sharing information and working together.

This cooperation is even spanning national boundaries, as in the Solway Firth Forum, which includes both Scottish and English members in its discussions. New channels have certainly been opened. But what is perhaps most exciting about these groups is that they are now wrestling with problems and possibilities relating to huge systems of sea, land and freshwater. Coastal walls in one place can have an impact on another; pollution and sediment from a river catchment can affect an estuary; change of saltmarsh can influence birds which travel to the next county, or country or continent.

So, although knowledge of the fine detail of places like estuaries is crucial to understand them, it is also necessary to try to see the bigger picture. At the very least, the CZM groups are now trying to glimpse that wider horizon.

If coping with changes wrought by rising water will be one challenge facing those with an interest in the coast in the next few decades, positively encouraging a state of flux on some other soft shores will also figure in their thinking. This applies particularly to sand dune systems, where there was a tendency in the past to protect the heaped-up sand from erosion, both from the sea, and from human feet and vehicles.

While untrammelled heavy access to dunes, by any mode of transport, would obviously be disastrous for most flora and fauna there, a modest level of disturbance can actually help to maintain the very conditions in which some scarce coastal wildlife thrives. This is because some of these creatures have a lifestyle suited to grabbing space on ground temporarily opened by windblow, then using the openings while they can as places to grow and reproduce, before other vegetation closes the gap. So keeping the variety of wildlife in a dune system high can be compatible with a reasonable level of public access, and can involve an acceptance of change as part of the natural way of things on these coasts.

Going with the flow on the shifting margins. Old Canute would give a friendly nod to that idea.

Above: Limpets and seaweed flourish in this rock pool on the Giant's Causeway in County Antrim.

Left: The blast of a winter storm hits the Gower coast in South Wales.

TEN MILLION WINGS

When darkness finally falls on Skomer, not long before midnight after a day of summer heat, we leave the old farm buildings and go out in search of banshees. It takes a while for our eyes to get accustomed to the gloom, and we stumble along trying to keep on the track more by feel than by sight. Although the shapes and colours and smells of this island have become familiar during the day, the character of the place has changed with nightfall.

Gull calls from bracken now deep in shadow, the touch of wind with a tang of saltiness on our faces, the faint sound of surf from somewhere far below; all have a heightened effect on our senses. The first glimpse of greeny-yellow light from a glow-worm hanging by the side of the path is startling in its strangeness, but as we walk on, and more and more of these pinpoints of phosphorescence seem to light our way, a new calmness eases in.

There are lights all around in the further distance – sulphur street lights of the coastal towns and villages, lights of the fishing boats out testing the waters of St Brides Bay, a blaze of arc lights and floodlights from the massed towers and pipeworks of the Milford Haven oil refineries. And above, the light from countless stars in a clear sky, the night before the summer solstice, with the white speck of a single satellite moving over.

A whoosh of air from unseen wings, skimming close and fast, breaks the reverie. A howling skirl which chills the blood follows; then there is stillness. We stand, scarcely daring to move or speak, peering at the sky and seeing nothing but stars. Then, from deep in the blackness of vegetation around us, wheezing calls begin.

Another howl, another rush of air, and we glimpse silhouetted wings as the shearwater announces its dramatic passage from sea to land – a screaming missile of a bird aiming for its summer home. More and more follow in quick succession, and within minutes, the air is busy with wings, the ground rustling with movement as wanderers return and their mates shuffle out to greet them.

The torch beam picks out two of them a few feet away, crouching dazzled and motionless in the glare, suddenly seeming much smaller and more vulnerable than the flying shapes suggest. But it does nothing to reveal the action beyond its beam, or over the next hummock, or beyond that to the ends of the island where the surface swarms with life.

Skomer, and its sister island of Skokholm, form the largest supercolony of manx shearwaters in the world. These islands lie close to the Dyfed coast, have had human visitors and residents for millennia, and through the writings of Ronald Lockley and many other ornithologists who followed, the seabirds here are among the best documented on earth.

The timing of their arrival back at breeding places, the kinds of nests they make, the number of eggs they lay, what they eat, how long they live, and a host of other details about their feeding, breeding and survival have been watched, weighed, measured and analysed. And yet what goes on here, as at all seabird colonies, is but a fragment of the totality for these creatures – a blip on a screen which stretches out across the ocean to the farthest horizon and beyond: and about which we know so little.

Even for the birds which visit such places in daylight hours, and whose activities are obvious above ground, there are precious few ways of understanding what happens when they lift off from the island's surface, fly out to sea and are lost to view over the element which is the mainstay of their lives. For the night visitors like these manx shearwaters, or their close relatives the tiny petrels – scarcely bigger than swallows – which flit in, bat-like, long after sunset, we know much less. Just attempting to calculate the size of their populations is fraught with difficulty.

But still we keep trying, like shining a flashlight in the dark. For we know that somehow, the fate of these birds – whose health depends on a summer harvest of marine life from the seas around our islands – may be linked to our own.

I click off the torch beam and we walk back down the track, with the Milky Way now a smoke of stars in the northern quarter, and a light still bobbing far out in the bay. What harvest are they getting there tonight, I wonder. What shoals have gone unseen?

Accurate counts at colonies are the foundation of attempts to understand the changing fortunes of seabirds. That sounds straightforward enough, but the reality is often mind-numbing in its necessary attention to detail, involving painstaking tallies in challenging land or sea conditions.

According to the most recent register of seabird colonies – carried out by the Seabird Group and the Nature Conservancy Council in the late 1980s – Britain and Ireland play host to some two-and-a-half million breeding guillemots, razorbills and puffins and more than two-and-a-half million pairs of other kinds of seabirds. Add immatures and other non-breeders, which in large colonies can swell summer numbers by thousands of birds, and a figure of more than ten million individual seabirds for these islands is not unreasonable.

Out of a world total of around 275 species, 24 different kinds of seabirds nest here regularly. The top three – guillemot, fulmar, and the dainty kittiwake – each top the million mark in terms of breeding birds alone. Next comes the puffin, then the manx shearwater. Perhaps surprisingly (for, to many people, large gulls seem synonymous with sea coasts and islands) the most numerous of that bunch – the herring gull – musters fewer than 200,000 pairs (less than one-third of the guillemot's breeding strength). At the other end of the scale,

Opposite: A colony of nesting gannets on Grassholm, part of the Pembrokeshire Coast National Park.

A grey seal pup — vulnerable to a hostile world.

the roseate tern – our scarcest seabird – barely scrapes in with a population that (in a good year) may number only 1,000 breeding birds – nearly half of which are clustered on one Irish island.

But concentration of breeders, be they scarce or abundant, is the normal state of reproductive affairs for many seabirds. Along much of our coastline, including most of England's eastern seaboard, you can travel for many kilometres without the merest hint of a seabird nesting site, let alone a colony. Availability of nesting places isn't the answer to their scarcity, for there are many likely looking seabird cliffs along the west coast with little more than a few gulls and shags to their name. Proximity to feeding grounds is the key.

Where the soup of microscopic marine life and sediments is stirred by currents which collide with islands, or hits the continental shelf, it gives a rich brew of fish and crustacea for seabirds to exploit. Just the stuff for helping chicks to change from fluffy nestlings to ocean wanderers in a few weeks of summer. But these conditions are special. As a rule of thumb, the further north and west you go on British and Irish coasts, the more likely you are to hit the magic sea mix. The Shetland Islands have the right blend in abundance, and the islands of the St Kilda group – our remotest archipelago – a superabundance.

St Kilda, where the shattered remains of a volcanic cone from Tertiary times poke from the ocean near the North Atlantic storm track, is home to the world's largest colony of gannets. More puffins breed here than anywhere else in Britain and Ireland. The great cliff of Connachair – Britain's largest sea cliff – and many other dizzying faces, host the largest,

oldest fulmar colony.

Add in the guillemots, the razorbills and gulls; the great skuas, or 'bonxies', which come to dive-bomb intruders in their territories; the shearwaters and petrels, including tens of thousands of Leach's petrels at one of their few eastern Atlantic locations. Finish with a sprinkling of tysties, those dapper-plumaged, carmine-footed guillemots of the inshore shallows, whose piping calls and whistles add delicate music to the island air, and it's easy to see why a visit to St Kilda is usually high on the wish-list for any birdwatcher with a hankering after seabirds, and many other people besides.

For St Kilda represents more than just an amazing cluster of seabirds and spectacular island scenery. It encapsulates, perhaps, the essence of what gives our seabird islands such allure. Visible from the nearest other land only on the clearest of days, girdled by turbulent waters and requiring time, commitment and luck to reach, its very presence seems a challenge. The seabirds, by that token, are an incredible bonus, but only part of what draws us to such places.

Another fascination can be the mystique of former inhabitants. For on so many islands where seabirds still thrive, people once eked out a living and then abandoned the struggle, leaving only deserted cottages and other stoneworks as reminders of their past occupation. The former villagers quit St Kilda in 1930, ground down by decades of emigration, disease, and spartan conditions.

Before that, harvesting seabirds was essential for the St Kildans, who were often cut off from contact with other people for many months each year. Each spring and summer, they killed tens of thousands, with fulmars, gannets and puffins the mainstay. Over many centuries of recorded history on St Kilda, it seems to have been a sustainable harvest, carried out with great skill and daring. Cragsmen dangled from horsehair ropes to snitch fulmars from ledges high above the sea, or leapt ashore on wave-skirted stacks to take gannets. They also placed their storage structures on flat ground and steep slopes alike. These buildings are now a testament in stone to their vanished culture.

Elsewhere, traditions of fowling and egging, which added some variety to the diet of coastal communities, have also gone. Only on the island of Sula Sgeir, north of Lewis, does an echo of the old ways remain in the autumn killing of a quota of gannet chicks, or 'gugas' by men from the township of Ness.

It is a toll which has been taken for at least as long as the many centuries for which records for this remote place exist. For the men who take part in it, a voyage and stay on Sula Sgeir seems to have an almost ritual significance – a rite of passage – with many superstitions and codes of behaviour governing their actions. For me, reaching this gannet-thronged place on a day of swirling sea fog felt like arriving at the ends of the earth. And I glimpsed, perhaps, just a little of what makes the ancient harvest here so important to the people of Ness.

Opposite: Small islands in the Pembrokeshire Coast National Park are home to many thousands of seabirds.

A release from the pressures of egging and fowling would have been a boon to Britain and Ireland's seabirds earlier this century, and certainly helped the gannet's still-continuing expansion. Ireland's Eye and Clare Island, Troup Head, Foula and Fair Isle have all been added to the gannet's domain in recent years, and overall, numbers have increased by tens of thousands since the 1960s. Good feeding conditions – including a ready supply of discarded fish from trawlers – may also have boosted seabird numbers; for most kinds of seabirds which breed here have shown great population increases this century.

But human capability to tip the scales of fortune against them, through oil spills, pollution and overfishing, still looms large. One of the pressure points in debate is so-called 'industrial' or 'biomass' fishing, where fish not sold directly for human consumption are caught for processing into meal and oil.

Sandeels – small, shoaling fish which are a staple food for many seabirds, and are also eaten by larger kinds of marine life, such as seals and porpoises – have been the focus of an industrial fishery in the North Sea since the 1960s. Roughly a million tonnes of sandeels are caught here each summer, most of which is processed into agricultural feedstuffs, with Danish fish farms a big market. For a while, oil from these fish was even used to fuel some Danish power stations.

Around Shetland, sandeel fishing was stopped between 1991 and 1994, after a run of disastrously poor seasons when many adult seabirds failed to find fish to feed their chicks. Since then, sandeels have come back in strength to Shetland waters, and most seabird chicks there are well fed again. A limited industrial fishery has now reopened, but no one can be sure how well the fishery, and the many seabirds which hunt the same prey, can coexist in future.

Elsewhere, such as in the Firth of Forth off eastern Scotland, huge sandeel catches – unrestricted by any quota – are being made close to eastern Britain's second largest puffinry. Each 750 tonne boatload from that fishery holds, by my reckoning, the equivalent of 75 million puffin foodloads (which weigh-in at around 10 grammes on the average chick-feeding run). Again, no one can say whether or not the human fishery is threatening the puffin's slice of sandeel action.

Oil pollution is the most visible of human-linked influences on seabirds. But surprisingly, most oil that pollutes the sea comes from land-based industries. High-profile accidents only account for about 10 per cent of the rest. Most ship-caused pollution is from the routine flushing of waste oil, both by ordinary boats cleaning their bilges and by tankers off-loading ballast.

After delivering a cargo of oil to a refinery, most tankers return empty to their supply port, but to do this safely, they need to take on water as ballast. New tankers have separate tanks for ballast and oil, but older tankers do not, so their jettisoned water is oily. It is still legal for ships to dump oil within 12 nautical miles of the coast – a cheap option for boat owners, but a vile one for the wildlife that falls foul of it. This chronic pollution takes its grim reaping of seabirds every day around the busiest shipping lanes, such as the English Channel.

But it is the megaspills which grab the biggest headlines – perhaps none more so in Britain and Ireland than the wreck of the M.V. 'Braer'. Pushed onto rocks near Shetland's southernmost headland, the stricken vessel disgorged twice as much crude as the infamous spill from the 'Exxon Valdez' – which devastated marine and coastal wildlife in Alaska's Prince William Sound. By some miracle of weather working, the gale which broke the 'Braer' also dispersed its pollution. Within two months of the wreck – just as hundreds of thousands of seabirds were returning to breed not far from where the hulk still lay – the island shores were clean of oil. The feared 'disaster' had become a mere 'incident', by some reckonings: its wildlife casualties minimal. Or had it?

In early 1996, three years after the Braer foundered, much prawn fishing and mussel gath-

Two of the many Russian 'klondiker' vessels which once came annually to Loch Broom in north-west Scotland.

Opposite: A puffin at one of its major British breeding grounds – the Farne Islands National Trust Reserve in Northumberland – about to deliver sandeels to a chick in a nearby burrow.

ering was still banned in Shetland, and fish had gone from large areas of seabed. For although the oil was out of sight, some of it could still smother life in the ocean depths. Many Shetlanders are now worried, as never before, about the future health of the sea which is the mainstay of both human life and wildlife on their islands.

They have good reason. For other events in early 1996 suggested that little had happened since the Braer's demise to lessen the risk, or the potential impact, of serious oil spillage on British and Irish coasts, despite more than 100 recommendations for change made by Lord Donaldson in an official inquiry which came in the Braer's poisoned wake.

When the 'Sea Empress' hit rocks on its approach to Milford Haven in Dyfed in February of that year, it eventually spewed out almost as much oil as the 'Braer' had done. But its impact was even greater. In the darkest period of the 'Sea Empress' emergency, in what the Countryside Council for Wales called 'the worst single oiling incident ever in British waters', oil stretched from Strumble Head in Wales to the beaches of North Devon, 120 kilometres to the south.

In just a few days, one of the most varied and life-rich coastlines in western Europe had been thoroughly tainted. Marine creatures of many kinds, both rare and common, suffered

These shags were two of the thousands of wildlife victims of the oil spill caused by the grounding of the Braer oil tanker in the Shetland Islands in 1993.

greatly, from the green rockpool starfish at one of its few British colonies, to the molluscs and shellfish along every shore and the thousands of seabirds and seaducks which were affected by the life-clogging pollution. Their populations are likely to take many years to recover, while tourism – one of the mainstays of the local economy, also reels from the shock.

Yet even here, in the vicinity of one of the busiest ports in Britain, there is still a chance that it could all happen again. For the lofty designations of a national park, heritage coast, many Sites of Special Scientific Interest and the marine nature reserves at Skomer and Lundy are no match for the power of a fuel industry eager to keep prices as low as possible to meet the ever-growing demand for its products. In the context of that expanding market-place and the fierce competition there, and in the absence of mandatory design and safety standards which could help to reduce the risk and the impact of tanker accidents, it is not surprising that coastal wildlife and rural communities become expendable pawns in the global oil game.

Double-hulled tankers, coastal radar for surveillance of shipping movements and powerful tugs ready to come to the assistance of vessels in distress could all help to lessen the risk of future massive spills. But these things cost megabucks, which both government and business seem reluctant to spend. Shetland, Pembrokeshire, the Minches, the English Channel – there but for the grace of some dice throws of weather and ageing hardware goes the oil again.

By the time of the 'Sea Empress' spill, media fatigue over oilspill stories had set in with a vengeance, and despite the magnitude of that event, it was difficult, after the first few days, to get detailed reports of its unfolding tragedy. It was as if, after a feeding frenzy on Shetland, the news media had become sated with crude.

Yet the pictures beamed from Shetland around the planet still stick in the mind like tar on feathers. The image of a seabird rescue worker, clad in yellow oilskins, face hidden in a breathing mask, plucking an oil-spattered casualty from a beach, has become a chilling icon of our times, making it plain, more acutely than ever, that even the farthest shores can be tainted.

If the icon has another side, it is that it emphasises that, even in the face of apparently insuperable odds, there are people willing to struggle for something better. I try to hold on to that idea, as I think of the seabirds returning to Skomer in the early summer, to strive to find fish near the local boats in the waters of St Brides Bay, as the big tankers pass close by. I try to remember how it was with the shearwaters. I try hard to believe that there are still some torchbeams in the dark.

Opposite Left: Trawlers attempting to clear oil leaked from the Sea Empress disaster in the approaches to the Bristol Channel in 1996.

Opposite Right: Sorting the catch in a small trawler in the Bristol Channel in 1995.

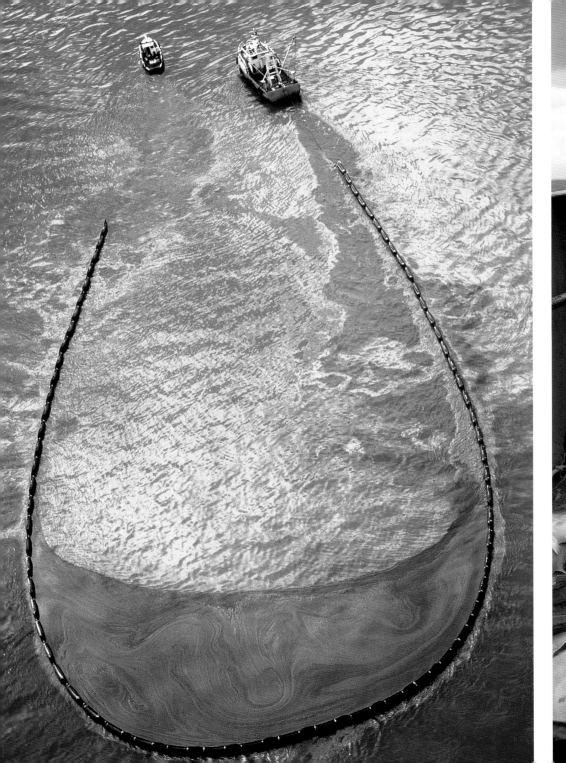

COARSE GRAIN, FINE GRAIN

In a darkened room within the Royal Airforce's research base at Farnborough in Hampshire, I sit peering at brightly coloured patterns on a television screen. My guide presses a button and the colours change, highlighting features that were obscure in the previous image. Then she pushes a joystick to the left and zooms in on the picture. I see the location of my house in northern Scotland and the pattern of the fields around it; notice where the hills give way to pasture, and where the old wood flanks the road.

We move rapidly over the landscape, as if seeing it from space; travellers over territory that is both familiar in shape, yet alien in colour. Switching to a neighbouring county, where there is less pasture and more crops, the arrangement of colour changes. Courtesy of a massive computer in another part of the building, which stores information beamed down from the LANDSAT satellite, we can take-in broad sweeps of country at a glance, compare and contrast different types of surface cover, define the boundaries of farms and wetlands, moors, mountains and a host of other features.

The pictures revealed by such high-tech scans allow stocktaking as never before of the precise layout of human uses of the land of Britain and Ireland. This is a kind of Domesday gallery – a databank for the new millennium, stored in code in microchips rather than scribed on vellum – and it shows with awesome accuracy just how great the influence of people has been on our home ground in the 6000 years or so since Neolithic settlers first began to make their mark on the forests which once cloaked these islands.

But a fundamental part of the picture has stayed prominent through the 1,000 years since the Norman stocktaking and several millennia before it. More than any other feature, whether natural or human-linked, agriculture dominates the British and Irish scene today, as it has done for hundreds of human generations. Farmland is the essential fabric of much of the land surface, the background within which other features are set.

This is obvious in many fertile plains. But even in the uplands, the fields, farm walls and buildings often form the foreground to the wilder land above them, much of which may also be within the compass of the agricultural scene through its use as rough grazing for sheep flocks. There is no escaping the influence of farming, as the most recent summary statistics compiled through programmes such as the Countryside Survey in England, Wales and Northern Ireland and Scottish Natural Heritage's National Countryside Monitoring Scheme, show.

In England, nearly two-thirds of the entire land surface is now tilled as arable to grow wheat or other crops, or maintained as grazed grassland. Ireland surpasses even this, with some 70 per cent of land in the Republic under grass and crops, and more than 80 per cent of Northern Ireland devoted to agriculture, principally through extensive, fertilized pastures. In Wales, farm grasslands and tillage cover more than half the country. Only in Scotland does the dominance of such intensive agriculture drop – to less than one third of the ground – but here there are vast expanses of sheepwalk on the upland heaths and coarse pastures, and some lowland counties, such as Fife, where over half the land surface is ploughed as arable.

Within this broad canvas of lands geared so closely to the production of food, the finer details can vary greatly from place to place, shaped by a host of influences – from geology and climate, to quirks of history. This variation is part of the very essence of what makes travel in Britain and Ireland so rewarding, in comparison to journeys in more uniform landscapes.

Typically, in the course of a few tens of kilometres, you can move from one type of rural

Opposite: Meadows full of buttercups surround traditional hay barns in Swaledale, within the Yorkshire Dales National Park.

Below: A vast, featureless potato prairie at Potterhanworth Fen in Lincolnshire.

scene to another, quite different, countryside. From the intimate, undulating small fields, thick with hedgerows and wound round with ancient lanes in the Welsh Marches, to the regular, fenced flatlands of the Cheshire plain; from the grainfields of Moray to the crofting fringe of the West Highland seaboard; from the fuchsia-rimmed smallholdings of Dingle to the great pastures of Limerick and Tipperary's Golden Vale – are journeys that can be made in a morning by modern transport, with the promise of more variety and more contrasts beyond them for the afternoon.

But within this huge range of agricultural scenes – still holding some distinctive local elements, despite the diversity-crushing pressures of market forces – some general themes emerge. Again, the scans from satellites, coupled with the efforts of teams of survey workers who go to record the crops, livestock, flora and fauna of selected farmscapes in great detail, reveal something of the geographical spread and content of the major farming patterns.

Landscapes devoted to the production of cereals and other crops cover more than one-third of Britain. These arable lands are concentrated mainly in the south and east – in East Anglia, the East Midlands and the Home Counties, with further swathes in the Central Valley and eastern lowlands of Scotland, and a lesser amount in south-east Ireland. This is the ground of wheat and barley, of oilseed rape and sugar beet, where summers are sunny, the rainfall low, and the underlying rocks generally soft and fertile, with chalks, clays and sediments the norm. With such a combination of pleasant climate and high productivity it is not surprising that the present arable landscapes were some of the first territory occupied by prehistoric settlers, and today girdle many of Britain's major cities.

Pastural landscapes, dominated by grasslands which are often thick with ryegrass and heavily fertilized, cover a great part of Ireland and are widely spread in England and Wales – stretching from the West Country in a broad band along the Welsh borders and across the West Midlands to Northumberland, around the Welsh seaboard and with a scattering on the low ground and eastern coastlands of Scotland. In England, Wales and Ireland, this

is hedgerow country *par excellence*, with little snow lie, moderate rainfall, and fairly fertile soils – the agricultural setting for most of the rest of the population outwith the arable areas.

Upland fringes and true uplands account for the rest of the land surface in agricultural terms. This is the ground which takes up most of the Welsh interior, the Highlands and Southern Uplands of Scotland, the Pennine chain and nearby high ground of the Lakes and northern English moors, and the western fringes of Ireland. The climate and soil are much harsher here – the rain heavy, winter chills long and snowfalls often deep, the geology built on volcanic rocks that spawn acid earth and food-poor grasses.

The uplands and their fringes are thin on hedges, but are threaded with fences and walls which mark out sparse grazings on heaths and rough grassland for the hill farmers who still eke out a precarious living here. Production of lamb is the mainstay of these farmers, and sheep in their millions have the run of the uplands. Add in the smallholdings of western Ireland, and the crofts in north-west Scotland, which have an intensive mixed farming activity, often on a part-time basis, and the general themes of British and Irish agriculture in the late 1990s are mapped out.

Despite their massive influence on the look of most of the land, farmers are now only a small minority of the population. Most people live in towns and cities and have no connection with agriculture, other than as consumers of its products. Even in rural areas, fewer than one in five residents is likely to have a farming connection.

In many families, the link with the land was severed a century or more ago, when the rise of urban-centred industries prompted great shifts of people from country to town. Yet the economic importance of agriculture, and its well-documented impact on more natural

Above: A barn owl rests from its nightly hunting.

Opposite: Laying an oat stook in a traditional 'hedge' walled landscape at Zennor in Cornwall.

vegetation cover and wildlife, makes the activities of the relatively small and still dwindling band of farmers a focus for intense debate.

One feature of this in the last two decades has been a polarization of views, where people worried by the continuing erosion of valued wildlife through the seeming relentless expansion and intensification of agriculture have been pitched into conflict with farming interests. Destruction of hedgerows, drainage of wetlands, grubbing-out of woodlands, overburning of moor grazings, pollution of watercourses and contamination of beef by feeding animal offal to cattle, are part of the depressing baggage of negative qualities which modern farming now carries with it. Yet knowledge of these negatives can all too often be combined with a characterization of the typical farmer as someone thriving both on the fat of the grainlands as a cereal baron, and on a gravy train of national and European subsidies.

The basic description of the variety of broad agricultural landscape types within Britain and Ireland should alone be sufficient to erase this caricature. Add further facts – that of over 200,000 farms in Britain, for example, around half are smallholdings of less than 50 acres and that a further 100,000 are medium-sized farms of less than 250 acres, with only a few thousand larger than that, and the stereotype wears even thinner. Look to the hills – where some 60,000 British upland farmers work, many in their mid-fifties or older, and where one in three survives precariously on profit of less than £5,000 per year, and a realization dawns that something very strange has happened in the relationship between farmers and non-farmers.

The profits of the few – arguably the one-fifth of the farmers who reap four-fifths of the available subsidies – and the actions aimed at maximizing food production, promoted by successive governments since the 1940s, have created a mythical monster – the farmer as an ogre in the eyes of some people who care deeply about loss of natural qualities in the countryside.

The gulf between town and country yawns wide now, yet there could be ways to bridge it. Part of that process could begin with an appreciation of just how much the rural scene has changed, not just in the few decades since the post-war push for agricultural efficiency and higher productivity, but many times before that. And as it has changed, so too has wildlife, so too have people.

In my own family, I am fortunate to still have a link with farming through my in-laws in Shropshire. But before marrying, the closest link was two centuries old, when forebears on my mother's side farmed in Ayrshire – beside the holding where Robert Burns and his brother worked the land.

The thought that my great, great, great grandparents could have chatted with the poet across a stone wall, or even heard some of the bard's thoughts about the wildlife on the farms, gives me a shiver of pleasure each time I contemplate it. For in one potent image I can conjure a personal and emotional link from what was, to what is; from the business of farming, to the enjoyment of nature – something that Burns at his best was so skilled at evoking in the closing years of the eighteenth century.

In farming terms, two hundred years is not so long – four working lifetimes of fifty years gets us back there. And yet the differences between successive fifty year periods during this time are enormous, both in terms of the look of the land and of human involvement with it.

In the late 1790s, Britain was locked in war with France. But against a background of dread of Bonaparte and fear of famine, farming was buoyant. The price of wheat was high, and rents and land values were rising, so even downland pastures were going under the plough. For decades, a spirit of agricultural 'improvement' had gripped larger landowners. A Board of Agriculture had been newly created, with Sir John Sinclair of Caithness – tireless compiler of agricultural and social statistics, and great force for reform of farming

Opposite: The epitome of the English countryside; an organically run Herefordshire apple orchard in full blossom.

Below: Traditional hedge laying in West Wales.

Enclosure fields and hedges in Carmarthenshire.

enclosure movement had gathered momentum, and surveyors were radically reshaping the farmscape. The last vestiges of the old open-field system of strip-farmed, communally-managed arable, which in some places had persisted for many centuries, were being swept away. In place of the curving boundaries and broad expanses of the open fields, a net of straight lines bounding smaller, rectangular enclosures was cast.

Some fifty years on, in the late 1840s, Victoria was in the second decade of her long reign, and fortune was beginning to smile again on lowland farming in Britain, despite a slump after the end of conflict with Napoleon. Rotational farming, often with cereals as the basis for a four-course rotation – from a root crop, through cereals to grass or peas, and back to cereals – was coming into its own. Great strides were being made in the development of cattle, sheep and pigs through selective breeding, and artificial fertilizers, such as superphosphate, were being used for the first time. Boosted by the new cropping patterns, brown hare numbers were increasing, while partridges were abundant along the margins of fields, including the recently enclosed ground where millions of hedging plants – especially hawthorn – were adding fresh shape to the lowlands and giving song perches by the billion for birds such as chaffinches and yellowhammers.

But in Ireland, the scene was one of devastation, in the black years of the Great Famine, when the potato crop, which had supported a rural population at a perilously high level, failed through blight. Widespread starvation, fever and mass emigration, pushed the number of Irish inhabitants down by two million from a pre-Famine peak of more than seven million. With this human tragedy as a background, the look of Irish land changed, as the smallest of smallholdings vanished, and the last vestiges of many woodlands (already reduced by centuries of felling) disappeared.

In northern Scotland and the Scottish islands, depopulation was also changing the face of many fertile straths and glens. Here, the blighted potato crop was but the final insult and injury for a peasantry oppressed for decades by landlords often more interested in profits from extensive sheep flocks than in the welfare of the small-scale farmers who were their tenants. These 'Clearances', where entire communities were obliterated to make way for sheep, often in circumstances of great cruelty, cast a blight on the Highlands which has persisted to this day, and whose bitter legacy can still be seen in the empty shells of cottages in glens where no crops grow, and where scarcely a human now lives.

The contrast between famine-ravaged Ireland, the sheep-smothered, depopulated Highlands and more fortunate areas in lowland Scotland, Wales and England at this time could hardly have been greater. Despite the gradual advent of new machinery, farming in the fertile lowlands was still a labour-intensive enterprise. Even at the end of the nineteenth century – after two decades of a slump in farm fortunes which would continue, with little

methods – as its dynamic first president.

The talk was of new grass mixes and crop rotations, of stock improvement, and of taming the 'wastelands' – reclaiming fertile ground from the bogs and moors. In the lowlands, the

Opposite Left: Ploughing the land and collecting unearthed stones in Denbighshire.

Opposite Right: The constant need for supplies of builder's sand and gravel threatens much agricultural land.

respite, until the 1940s, whole villages were still strongly hefted to the business of farming. From the blacksmith who made the tools, mended machinery and shod the heavy horses, to farmhands, ploughmen, carters, shepherds, and yeomen, and a host of others, including women and children who would help at harvest or at seedtime, hand-hoe the root crops or thresh the grain, farming was a community-based activity.

A new pattern had already emerged in the depopulated British uplands, where a fall in prices for hill sheep, prompted by cheap imports of wool from New Zealand late in the century, had fuelled the rapid rise of the sporting estate, devoted to the pursuit of grouse and deer (see 'Purple Passage'). That expansion brought the downfall of many predators. Wildcat and pine marten, buzzard and many other kinds of birds of prey were pushed to the edge of oblivion – or over it – by zealous gamekeepers, keen to remove any competition for traditional quarry on estate ground.

It also underscored the severing of communal links with the ground now used to cultivate a crop of game for culling by the chosen few. This was a bitter twist of fortune in the Highlands, especially, where such lands had once been held as common property by clansfolk.

But it also drove a wedge between the land and people in many other places, through the denial of access to some of the highest, wildest areas, and by fostering an attitude of antagonism between urban, mass interests and rural, elitist interests. This has persisted even to this day (when some splendid places in the British uplands are still, legally but incredibly, treated as the private preserve of those who hold title to their land and view them as sanctuaries for a handful of game species, not part of the common inheritance of the nation).

Fifty years on again – to the late 1940s – and the world had emerged, bomb-shocked, from a six-year conflict of monstrous severity. Food was in desperately short supply in Europe, but (with the image of the mushroom cloud now burned on modern consciousness) confidence was brimming in the power of science and new technology to alter for good as well as ill, to change scarcity to plenty.

The push for greater production of home-grown food, which had gathered speed during the war years, now zoomed into the fast lane. New machinery, new chemicals and new government subsidies gave it financial clout and a technical turbo-boost. Britain and Ireland wanted farmers to succeed – to move from digging for victory to growing for prosperity – and the farmers rose to the challenge as never before.

There was no shortage of innovations to help this process and speed the plough. The little Ferguson tractor, whose brilliantly simple three-way linkage could be coupled to a host of implements, literally opened up new possibilities, making even high and stony ground tractable. Routine operations – such as ploughing, harrowing, seeding and cutting – became quicker, and the winning of new farmland beyond the fringes of the old became an attractive proposition.

The plough's machine-drawn furrows knew few bounds. Old woodlands, downland turfs,

flower-rich hay meadows, heaths, bogs and fens – all could be converted to arable with relative ease. Felling, draining, ploughing and reseeding became the order of service in the new agricultural crusade, with a copious sprinkling of strange liquids as the wonder stuff to bless its all-changing advance.

As crop-enhancing fertilizers and insect- and weed-zapping sprays came on stream, tractor-mounted equipment allowed their speedy delivery to the fields. Chemicals and machines seemed made for each other. And if the old agricultural landshapes were too irregular or narrow to suit the new regime, that could easily be remedied.

Some recently developed machines, such as the combine harvester – the first self-propelled model of which appeared in Britain in 1940 – were too large to negotiate the entrances and turn within the confines of the old, small fields. So fields and their gateways were expanded to accommodate them.

Incentives for further change – to transform and take more and more land in agricultural hand – came thick and fast. From guaranteed prices ushered-in by the 1947 Agriculture Act onwards, to the subsidies deluged from the European Community's Common Agricultural Policy, from the propaganda of marketing boards to the techno-fixes peddled by legions of advisers, the thrust was the same: dominate the land and subjugate the wild and there were rich rewards, ripe for the reaping, by the forward-looking farmer.

It was a message which could still ring true until the 1960s, when Rachel Carson's 'Silent Spring' sounded the first international notes of alarm about agrochemicals, and the near extinction of otters and peregrines on British ground brought the poisoned legacy home to roost. By the 1970s, concerns about losses of other wildlife and their living spaces were gaining popular currency, boosted by the rapid expansion of bodies such as the Royal Society for the Protection of Birds.

By the 1980s, surveys of land cover, assisted by methods such as satellite-based remote sensing, were being used in a big way. The new technology confirmed the scale of changes wrought by the old, and the burgeoning green lobby condemned the sins of the agricultural fathers and the offspring who still sought to follow in their tractor ruts.

The all-conquering heroes, who rode high on the tractors of the post-war push for foodstuffs, had delivered the goods and then some, but were now cast as villains by many of the adults from a baby boom which they had helped to nourish. It was a cruel irony, for, coupled with the gloomy catalogues of wildlife and wild places in decline, there had also been a fundamental change in the nature of occupation of rural areas. In its way, despite the machines and sprays and scientific back-up now available, this has made modern farmers themselves a rare, and in some places an endangered breed – often working in an isolation which is far from splendid.

With the disappearance of most of the trades and skills which once made-up the farming community, and with the severing of close ties to the life of villages and towns in the farmlands, much more has been lost than just the techniques of different kinds of work. A whole way of relating to the land has gone too, which, for all the seeming quaintness which may now colour its former details, at its best reflected a sensitivity to the nuances of place – an awareness of what made the very stuff of the soils and seasons and crops of one area different from those in another, and why a pride in a particular farm and its parish could matter in the human scheme of things.

The solitary farmer, riding a tractor across fields where perhaps only one other person, often a family member, is employed, may represent a pinnacle of achievement in one sense – the mastery of the elements of food production and economy of labour. But it is an image whose loneliness brings home the realization that such efficiency is not all that should be reckoned on the balance sheet of a healthily farmed countryside. Other values – of community with ourselves, and community in terms of human awareness and linkage to the land and its natural processes – also matter. The diversity of all kinds of life, including our own, has dwindled on the farmlands.

Restoring more variety again, in ways that will offer real scope for work relevant to current needs, and not merely be an action replay of some heritage themes, will take money and vision. Neither of these is necessarily in short supply when the farmed countryside is being considered. Publically accountable money through government and EU subsidies is poured into farming, but its channelling is still directed primarily to production.

With expenditure on the Common Agricultural Policy in Britain alone now running at a whisker short of £3 billion each year, only about 3 per cent of which is spent on environmental measures, there is ample room for change. Local knowledge could play a crucial part in this, helping to reduce tensions inherent in a system where key agricultural policy decisions are made at EC level, but where environmental objectives demand (but do not receive) maximum sensitivity to local variations, right down to the level of individual farms and fields.

Some of the practicalities of helping wildlife to regain lost ground in farmland are now well documented, and some of the hardware now available to mollify the impact of chemicals is awesome. Weedkillers and crop boosters can now be sprayed with pinpoint accuracy, helped by on-tractor computers and satellite-signalled positioning, by those who can afford the microchips. But the story of the last few decades suggests that science and gadgetry alone can be dangerous allies for farming if uncoupled from a sense of wider connections.

'I'm truly sorry man's dominion has broken nature's social union,' wrote my great-great-great grandparents' neighbour to a mouse he had disturbed in its nest when ploughing in the autumn of 1785. Several generations later, there are many, many people – farmers and conservationists alike – who must feel the resonance of these words and sense their challenge.

A gorse-covered hillside in Denbighshire.

BEYOND THE WASTELAND

The process begins before dusk has darkened the sky in the long months of autumn and winter. First arrivals go largely unnoticed. Outriders of the main mass, they circle and settle on high ledges. With gathering twilight, many more come after the vanguard. Their presence becomes audible – a chatter of small voices, like scrambled code over the traffic noise, a swirl of wings in the sky. Flock after flock homes in from suburbs and from distant fields, making for the city centre as commuters head for trains that will carry them in the opposite direction.

The starlings' aerobatics are spellbinding. Turning as one, several hundred rise and fall, swerve and circle, above multi-storey offices, shops and apartments. Now strung like a dark plume of smoke, now packed in a spinning orb, now a giant amoeba, the flocks flash an unpredictable semaphore – anarchic in sequence, yet structured in detail – in counterpoint to the monotonous regularity of neon lights, sodium lights, traffic lights and tail lights at street level.

The grand finale comes with a flourish, as it usually does. Streaming downwards in a seeming crash-dive, the members of the air display team hurtle for the buildings. Each must pull up in the last split second before impact for a precision touchdown on a ledge, two or three floors above the street. But this manoeuvre is hard to see. All I know, as I stand still and look up for a short while from the pavement, jostled by pedestrians unused to such aberrant behaviour, is that the buildings have now been transformed. A wild spirit has breezed into the city on the night air, and I thrill to the sound and the sight of it.

For most of us in Britain and Ireland, as in much of western Europe and North America, our most regular encounters with wildlife are in urban and industrial settings, for that is where the great majority of us spend the bulk of our lives. We might hanker after the plants and creatures which could be seen in summer fields, windy coasts, purple moors, or a great sweep of mountain plateau, but precious few of us have the chance to experience such places on anything like a frequent basis, let alone enjoy daily contact and immersion in their intricacies.

Ireland has the closest links with its rural roots, for its population came late to this state of town and country affairs. It wasn't until the late 1960s that the majority of its people could be classed as urbanites – a radical shift from the turn of the century, when less than one-third of the people in the Republic, for example, lived in cities.

In Britain, the move away from the land to people the stone and brickscapes began generations earlier, with an exodus which gathered momentum in the late 1700s and accelerated to a flood through the 1800s and beyond. By the close of Victoria's reign in 1901, four out of every five people in England and Wales, and more than two-thirds of Scots, lived in towns and cities. At the same time, the population of more than 70 British towns had topped the 50,000 mark, and several densely populated areas, from Clydeside to London, were spreading to merge with each other as 'conurbations' – large tracts of land dominated by industry and housing, and functioning as massive, non-rural, economic and social units. The process has continued through this century, further cemented by the rise of suburbia, creation of new towns, and headlong decline of the rural workforce.

Scarcely 250 years have passed since the Industrial Revolution – which propelled such shifts in location and work – got up a real head of steam. But the infrastructure which sustained and boosted industrial growth and change from then onwards, the abandoned workings that fuelled it, and the very fabric of towns and cities whose expansion was linked to it, are now firmly on the map for wildlife. Canals, railways and roads; pits, quarries and spoil heaps; walls and roofs; cellars and attics; as well as the more obvious living spaces of gardens and parks, are territory which wildlife, able to cope with sometimes extreme conditions of soil chemistry and proximity to people, can exploit to its advantage.

These riches are more than oddities on the British and Irish scene, fascinating simply because they demonstrate natural resilience in the face of unnatural odds. The greening, furring and feathering of places where the very bowels of the earth may have been exhumed in times past, and where bricks, concrete and asphalt smother all traces of soil, does have great symbolic value. But it is also the stuff of most people's everyday experience of nature, and, as such, adds a vitality – often surprising, unplanned and unpredictable – to the more routine shapes and schedules of urban existence.

Even one or two creatures breaking through the city limits to try some street life can make a mark on many people's thinking, perhaps helping them to further relish their own position as citizens. As a schoolboy in Glasgow in the late 1960s, I well remember how thrilled I was at the news that peregrine falcons – then a species being pushed off the map in many counties by poisoning from agrochemicals in their prey – had taken up residence in one of the towers of Glasgow University. This was exciting enough, but the real tingler came with reports that one of the birds had started to target pigeons above the city's main shopping streets, but didn't always clinch its high-powered strikes.

So tales of pedestrians being stopped in their tracks when a headless pigeon fell to the pavement at their feet were just about plausible. Apochryphal or not, such stories had an allure which helped me to revel in encounters with the city's wildlife, and even boosted my civic pride. For they gave a strong sense of alternative ways of structuring the world – an

Opposite: Alders on the banks of the Brecon and Monmouth Canal.

antidote to uniformity; a refreshment for the soul. Nowadays, although immersed in rural life (but with multiple strands of high-tech communications systems to link me with many cities), I can relate very readily to the passions expressed by urban dwellers for their local wildlife.

This is easy when speaking to people involved in watching or guarding peregrines, such as the birds which have reclaimed old ground in Bristol after decades of absence, but can apply to thinking about much more widespread creatures. I also envy Bristol dwellers their streetwise foxes; Dubliners and Dundonians their city centre pied wagtail roosts; Sheffield inhabitants their canal-side fig trees; the burgers of Edinburgh their squirrels in Princes Street gardens; Londoners their ring-necked parakeets in the suburbs and pigeons in the squares; and Belfast citizens their chance to see kingfishers on the Laggan in the centre of town.

Yet, in using the possessive 'their', I am aware of a tension. It seems the correct term to use to express the psychology of positive human feelings about urban wildlife – a sense of shared citizenship. But another, and perhaps deeper, attraction of urban wildlife comes from the vanishingly thin or non-existent threads of human control and possession of such creatures – a sense of freedom and surprise at other life forms, which can be as intoxicating in an inner city as on the outer limits of a remote island.

The props and paraphernalia of trade and industry have helped wildlife to find chinks in the mortar since the earliest days of the industrial boom. Abraham Darby had lit the spark with his coal-fired ironworks at Coalbrookdale in Shropshire in 1709, but it was a flurry of inventions much later in the century – such as James Watt's rotary steam engine, and Hargreaves' Spinning Jenny – which really fanned the furnaces of white-hot growth. With production of goods – such as textiles, cast iron and pottery – now more concentrated in space and efficient in time spent per unit of manufacture, (whatever the costs in sweatshop toil), than ever before, distribution of raw materials and finished products to and from the new factories was crucial to continuing success.

Canals were the first superhighways of the new order, offering relatively safe, smooth transportation in times when long-distance road travel could be a muddy, pot-holed nightmare of jolting coaches and broken wheels. The first, created by the Duke of Bridgewater to link his collieries to Manchester, opened in 1761. By the middle of the next century, 8,000 kilometres of waterways linked the great estuaries of the Mersey, Severn, Trent and Thames; a connection helped by the low watersheds between their river basins.

The hook-up of mines and ironworks, mills and cities was the key to prosperity for those who could invest in such infrastructure to boost their businesses. When Josiah Wedgwood dug the first shovelful of earth to start the Trent and Mersey Canal in 1756, he was displaying, not just a token solidarity with Black Country working folk, but a canny appreciation of where some of the smart money would go and come from in decades to come.

In Ireland, development of the island's marvellously wide-ranging navigations, based on rivers joined by canals, was spurred by the desire to keep surplus parliamentary revenue within the island. But lower investment in industry there, due to political unrest, meant that canals never really came on stream as moneymaking concerns. Scotland's few canals also had only limited scope for tobacco barons and others to profiteer before the next big thing in communications – railways – burst onto the scene.

In 1840, there was still only some 7,500 kilometres of railway track in the world – most of it in Britain, Belgium and the USA. But by 1900, tens of thousands of kilometres had been strung across Britain and Ireland alone, much of it supported on large earthworks raised by legions of navvies (250,000 of whom had been at work here in the mid-1800s). Coverage of the uplands was patchy, but in England, there was scarcely a spot more than a few kilometres from a railtrack at the century's turn.

Within a single generation, tracks and stations, goods yards and sidings had transformed many urban landscapes, linked town and country, engulfed nearly 250,000 acres and prepared the way for the spread of suburbs and commuting on a grand scale. Railways allowed national bonding of economy and people in ways hitherto impossible, shrinking the divide of journey and haulage times between once-distant places, and eventually providing the means for the masses of urban workers to push beyond their usual bounds on holidays, and head for the burgeoning seaside resorts.

Reaching for a drawer, I lift out my great-grandfather's pocket watch. 'Presented to George Taylor by his fellow workmen in the carriage department, Caledonian Railway Works, St Rollox 15.5.15,' reads the inscription, etched in flowing script on its gold-plated base. The chance of steady work and a better life for his family would have brought him from Wick, near the northern limit of the British mainland, to Glasgow – one of the industrial powerhouses of the Empire – last century, I think. But what journeys, what exports, what loves and partings, what connections of people and place, did the skill of this Caithness emigrant, and many more like him, make possible?

More than eighty years on, I can only guess at these things. Yet I can still feel a link with the railways of my great-grandfather's day through some of the corridors, created to carry his craftsmanship, now severed from what remains of the national British railway network after the cuts of the 1960s.

Such old railway lines are often called 'disused', but for wildlife, walkers and cyclists, they have simply shifted use, often providing green-fringed avenues through otherwise difficult territory. Whether near car-choked streets or hedgerow-starved fields, they have been moved from one set of connections to provide linkages in others. Even the embankments of still-functioning railway lines can give food, shelter and cover to many kinds of wildlife, allowing creatures like urban foxes to make their moves from den to garden and back again in relative safety, or adding the flowers of May or the song of a whitethroat as

Opposite Left: Mining waste is the seedbed for this orchid-rich grassland in South Wales.

Opposite Right: Ox-eye daisies, weld and other wild flowers thriving on industrial waste near Wigan in Lancashire.

a summer gift to their environs.

Canals too, both used and unnavigable, give ribbons of possibilities – lifelines in sometimes sterile-seeming surroundings. When spared the excesses of brutalist channel 'management', and allowed a fringe of vegetation in the water and by towpaths, canals can be havens for plants, birds and insects, best appreciated (like many other waters) at an easy drift from a slow moving boat, or in a leisurely amble at the side. Canal-dwelling wildlife is often readily watchable, being well-used to the passage of humans in the confines of its narrow living space.

A walk which I made many times in the 1980s was along the side arm of the Grand Union Canal between Aylesbury and Bulbourne, on the borders of Hertfordshire and Buckinghamshire. The purpose of those promenades was to gather information for the British Trust for Ornithology's Waterways Bird Survey, but the pleasure came as much from the diversity of life which I encountered as from the data I entered on my survey maps.

Swans and kingfishers, reedmace and sedges, water voles and shrews, willows and poplars, and everywhere an abundance of moorhens – swimming jerkily across still water, calling from reed clumps, skulking under hawthorn boughs where their eggs lay cupped (to be pointed out from the towpath by Tiree, my keen-nosed Munsterlander dog) are abiding images of that offshoot of the artery which gave a reliable link between production centres in Manchester in the north and London in the south. Those, and the brightly decorated narrow boats – also taking the journey at a gentle pace – which were moored by the canalside pub at the Bulbourne end.

Water is a vital part of other important cast offs from industry, in former gravel workings left to flood, and in functioning reservoirs. Both of these can have a role as living space for wildfowl, fish and amphibians, and provide recreation for people through angling, watersports, or straightforward enjoyment of the scene from the bankside. Most of lowland England's biggest water bodies are flooded mineral workings or reservoirs which have been created this century. The area of flooded gravel pits tops 10,000 hectares, with several hundred hectares more added each year, while the area of reservoirs in mainland Britain probably covers some 14,000 hectares, around half of which has been flooded since the mid-1960s.

The benefits these waters now give (albeit that some, especially upland reservoirs – such as the notorious Cow Green – were created by inundating ground which would have better been left unflooded) can be seriously compromised. Conflicts arise between different users – such as between windsurfers and wildfowl watchers, anglers and canoeists – and through the limited scope for breeding and sheltering space for wildlife in abandoned pits where no thought has been given before flooding to providing islands and vegetation cover. But the best of them harbour a surprising richness of creatures, especially different kinds of waders, ducks and geese.

Spoils, piled high or spread thin, give support to other kinds of species – especially plants which can tolerate the difficulties of water shortage and chemical overdose. Trees such as birches can be able colonisers, jumping in to turn bare hills of waste material to new woodlands in remarkably short periods of time when conditions suit them. Orchids are also adept at making the challenge of harsh ground an opportunity for expansion, boosted by lack of competition.

At Knowsley on Merseyside, orchids occur in several areas which have been heavily modified by activities such as top soil removal or the spreading of pulverised fuel ash. The finest of these orchid havens is Kraft Meadow, part of one of the largest industrial estates in Europe and adjacent to a dual carriageway. Now run as a nature reserve under the care of the local borough's Countryside Ranger Service, Kraft Meadow hosts common spotted and southern marsh orchids (which can interbreed to produce huge cherry-red-flowered hybrids), early marsh, twayblade, and bee orchids – an impressive list for anywhere and a feast for the eyes of local schoolchildren who come to see the show on ranger-guided summer walks.

Glasgow is well blessed by orchids, with helleborines a local speciality. Broad-leaved helleborine is at home in a surprising variety of locations here. These have been carefully catalogued, by botanist Jim Dickson, as including parks, cemeteries, golf courses and gardens (between them the most commonly occupied spots), woodland, bushy areas along railways, bings (spoil heaps), quarries, meadows and roadsides. Two others are much rarer.

Young's Helleborine was first identified as a species in 1982 from plants in Co. Durham. Discovered in Glasgow in 1985 on a bing which has since been excavated for a landfill, it still survives precariously at another bing. This is currently its only known Scottish site. It shares this with the Dune helleborine, which is typically a scarce coastal dweller, but has a few inland sites – all of them on bings.

Above: Roosting starlings fly, locust-like around Runcorn Bridge on Merseyside.

Opposite: Chamomile and cornflower meadows in Bolton have been created by local residents and the Lancashire Wildlife Trust.

The abandoned remains of steel-making machinery on industrial wasteland at Dowlais, near Merthyr Tydfil in South Wales.

This is heady stuff – the rare and the endangered, fragile strangers in a strange landscape – but it is a sidetrack from the main buzz of wildlife in such city territory. For many people, this has more to do with the pleasures of encountering and encouraging more widespread species as part of their neighbourhood scene, perhaps spiced with a dash of the exotic from time to time.

Pioneering work by W. B. Teagle in the West Midlands, more than twenty years ago, helped to bring this philosophy to the fore. He showed that the Black Country – previously a byword for extremes of industrial activity (dark satanic mills and all) – was an excellent area to watch wildlife and that local people could help to foster its needs. Teagle's work sparked the formation of the first Urban Wildlife Group, when one of the wildlife-rich areas he had identified was destroyed.

From that small beginning, enthusiasm for urban wildlife spread rapidly, spawning hundreds more groups; prodding local authorities to fund urban ecology studies; helping a host of local nature reserves, community woodlands and wildlife gardens to get established; boosting efforts to clear rubbish from ponds, canals and rivers; and, quite simply, helping thousands of people in urban areas throughout Britain and Ireland to get back in touch with some natural elements of their surroundings.

Diverse, dynamic, highly energetic and enthusiastic – the urban wildlife devotees have been in the forefront of seeing conservation as something which brings people and wildlife together, rather than as a process which relegates each to their respective ghettoes, one marked 'town', the other labelled 'country', or 'reserve – keep out'.

Community, coordinated local action and a keen awareness of the nuances of place are all part of this new urban spirit of the post-industrial age. The starlings would love it.

Above: Common terns nesting near Shotton steelworks in North Wales.

Opposite: Hawthorn in bloom on coal mining waste in the Black Country of the West Midlands.

TOUCHING THE EARTH AGAIN

Out from the window, by the table where I write, the view has many facets. In the garden, spring bulbs are pushing green spears of new growth through winter-browned grasses. This ground was once a field, and before that, a heath. When common gulls land in the neighbouring pasture to forage for worms after rain, their calls hold an echo of the colony that was based here many years ago.

A clump of rowan trees is prominent near the garden's end. Still bare of leaves and with berries stripped, months earlier, by fieldfares that breezed in from the sea, plundered, then were gone, the filigree of trunks, branches and twigs is grizzled with lichens.

The first family to live in the cottage that once stood near them might have planted the eldest tree, perhaps as a charm to keep further misfortune from their door after arrival from another home in a distant glen, from which they had been evicted to make way for sheep. Beyond the rowans, a birchwood cloaks a terrace on the downward slope. Multi-stemmed, its coppiced trees were last cut beyond the memory of anyone now living hereabouts.

In the valley below, recent ploughing has carved out blocks of rich earth within the confines of fields whose boundaries were laid down in the land enclosures of nearly two centuries ago. Other pieces in the straight-edged mosaic hold muddy rectangles where pigs snout about near corrugated shelters, and greenswards where sheep and cattle graze. Many new houses have been built on that sunny slope in the last few years, some adding stables and horses to the area for the first time in decades. For this is prime commuter territory now, and ripe for conversion to paddocks by those with the time and money to spare for horsification.

Further north, an oil rig is anchored in the waters of the Firth, waiting until a shift in global prices makes its hardware in demand again out in the deeps. It dwarfs the strip of mudflat and saltmarsh on the far shore, which is squeezed between an industrial estate and the sea, and is scarcely visible at high tide beside the neighbouring town. Above the urban wedge, swathes of conifer plantation zig-zag among hill farms, stopping short only on the highest ground, where snow still clings to the moorland at the skirts of a cloud-girt mountain.

I can never weary of this view, or ascribe straightforward values to it. For I am keenly aware of my good fortune at being able to look out on its richness, day after day. There are precious few places in Britain and Ireland which combine such variety within a single scene, yet almost every part of it owes its current form to human enterprise and shaping. Some of this is ancient (although you have to look hard for the signs of the farmers who came here in Neolithic times), but much was carried out within the last two centuries, and most within the last fifty years.

In that sense, the vista, in its broad sweep, is little different from landscapes in many other parts of these islands, most of which have been drastically altered in the course of a few generations, as have the activities within them. A locally resident time traveller, beamed here from the late eighteenth century, would find little that was instantly recognisable in the view from my window, and would be baffled by the methods of farming, forestry, energy consumption and transport practised within it.

Yet some of the wildlife here has persisted through great lengths of time, and in both the general and the particular aspects of that survival, this scene is utterly different from so many other places. The lichens which cling to the trees can do so because airborne pollution has not poisoned them, either through the sulphurous fumes of earlier industry, with the carbon dioxide of massed vehicles or the nitrogen-steeped vapours of crop sprays. Out in the fields, skylarks and grey partridges are still part of the scene, and finches and buntings flock near cattle sheds and turnip rows. For this is an area of mixed agriculture, not swamped by any one form of crop or animal production.

A few tongues of native woodland – some ancient – roll along ridges and beside burn gullies, bringing thick greenery and tall, natural structure close to scattered houses and clustered settlements alike. Voles and wood mice – prey for foxes and owls – can use these as covered routeways through the farmland, as can scarcer creatures. Wildcats and pine martens are gaining new ground here, pushing out from the plantations which gave them scope to move from smaller refuges, where they had retreated from earlier persecution.

Such details are important. For although so much has been altered here through the enterprise of people, there is still scope for wildlife, not just to cling on by its toenails against the odds, but to thrive and change. It could be better – much that once lived here has gone with the reshapings – but it could be much worse. For variety – of wildlife, land cover and human activity – is still of the essence here, the spice that makes me relish life in this particular parish.

That mixture, and the intimacy of association between wildlife and people, has been much reduced in so many other areas, as chapter after chapter in this book has documented. Complete alteration or destruction of certain types of place is one measure of that loss. The

Opposite Left: Inner city children playing on a steel sculpture of a tree in Handsworth, Birmingham.

Opposite Right Top : Landfill garbage tips attract large numbers of gulls.

Opposite Right Below: Many people travel by car before going for a country walk. Parked cars at Malham in the Yorkshire Dales National Park.

details of the changes which have happened, particularly since the 1940s, are numbing.

During that time, nearly every single broad category of long-established wildlife haven in Britain and Ireland has been fragmented, altered in character, damaged or pushed virtually to oblivion. Plant- and insect-rich grasslands, whether in lowland meadows, downland turf or coastal grazings have, together with raised bogs, been amongst the hardest hit. But ancient woodlands, heaths of all kinds, wetlands and soft shores have also suffered greatly, as have the many rivers severed from their floodplains by the brutalities of attempted channel taming. Even rocky shores – seeming bastions of persistence over aeons of changes – have been tarred by a brush with the late twentieth century, the threat of massive oil pollution being an increasing menace along much of their length.

As such places have been shrunk and shattered, a host of wildlife has felt the shock. But the attrition goes much wider, taking in the agricultural ground, whose promotion in particular forms has been the driving force for many of the major reshapings of recent decades. Within the farmlands which have been the dominant land feature of much of Britain and Ireland for millennia, the variety of life – already much reduced by changes in the middle of this century – has fallen even further in the last twenty-five years or so.

In that time, more than half the skylarks in the UK have vanished, for example; as have four out of five grey partridges, three quarters of the farmland song thrushes and many of the lowland waders that once added their loud voices to the farmland scene. Brown hares are scarce or extinct in many of their old haunts, and many butterflies have disappeared from field margins. Cornfield flowers and other colourful arable 'weeds' are now a thing of the past in most places. Recent statistics show that the number of different plant species in arable fields and grazed ground, in both uplands and lowlands, has shrunk even since the late 1970s, during which time hundreds of thousands of kilometres of hedgerows and countless small ponds have vanished from British and Irish farmscapes.

I reach for a large dictionary, published in 1992. This was the year of the 'reform' of the Common Agricultural Policy, which has since done little to reduce the intensity of arable farming in the European Union, and of the advent of 'set-aside', which now offers scant prospect, in either its extent or content, of reversing the decline of embattled wildlife. I search for the word 'biodiversity', but cannot find it.

The omission seems a fitting one, given the ill-starred events of that year, and it emphasizes how recently the term was coined. In some ways, its absence is briefly appealing. For already the word slips all too easily from the lips of officials and governments who wish to make politically correct, rather scientific-sounding noises, but who do little to promote the measures which should follow from them. Like 'sustainable development', the jargon is near enough to comprehension to be acceptable, but far enough from tight definition in particular circumstances to give civil servants a welter of escape routes from action.

For I remember that 1992 was also the year of the much-hyped Earth Summit in Rio De Janeiro, where 153 signatories, including representatives of Britain, the Republic of Ireland and the European Union, signed 'The Convention on Biological Diversity'. This was followed, in 1994, by the UK government's 'Biodiversity: the UK Action Plan', whose overall goal was stated as being: 'to conserve and enhance biological diversity within the UK and to contribute to conservation of global diversity through all appropriate mechanisms'.

Fine sentiments, shame about the follow up. For in the years since then, many of the signs are, that at government level, both the UK and the Republic of Ireland have singularly failed to stop the attrition of life forms in their domains, and have even acted in ways guaranteed to deplete, rather than conserve, natural variety.

The plight of so-called 'special' wildlife sites is a telling case in point. In Ireland, bureaucratic bungling has been the recent bane. Ironically, this stemmed from attempts by the Irish government to tighten-up wildlife protection and identify sites for the EU-wide 'Natura 2000' network. This system aims to conserve the most endangered species and many prime wildlife places through the designation of what are termed 'Special Areas of Conservation' and 'Special Protection Areas', based on lists submitted by member states.

As a first step in this process, the Irish Office of Public Works carried out a nationwide survey to pinpoint possible 'Natural Heritage Areas', to replace previously designated 'Areas of Scientific Interest'. Unfortunately, the immediate upshot of this bamboozling welter of terminology was the destruction of many good wildlife areas before the EU even got wind of them. This happened because landowners were notified of possible NHA sites on their ground before legislation was in place to safeguard them. The more unscrupulous simply ploughed, planted, drained or burned, to reduce the wildlife interest and remove the threat of tighter controls on their activities. It was a blow by the few against the national and international aspirations of the many, with wildlife the out-and-out loser.

In the UK, the situation is even worse. For here, recent government action suggests that even those areas designated under UK law as 'special' for wildlife may only have this protection for as long as no one can think of a better use for them, or for as long as the nation is prepared to pay through the nose to prevent them being damaged. Britain currently has nearly 6,000 'Sites of Special Scientific Interest', which cover approximately 8 per cent of the land surface. By one token, those places are Britain's prime storehouses of biological variety. Plunder or destroy them, and the national reserve of that variety dwindles. Yet that is exactly what happens, year after year, as hundreds of these 'SSSIs' are damaged or disappear.

What's more, the conservation of such areas is handled through what is, both literally and metaphorically, a protection racket. Through this, in return for doing nothing, owners of SSSIs can be compensated for profits foregone through not carrying out operations which could damage the value of the sites. Some have benefited to the tune of £1 million or more in payments made in recent years.

It's a situation ludicrously at odds with the law protecting, say, listed buildings, where owners have a duty to maintain buildings in an agreed state of repair. Imagine the outcry if the Church of England announced that it wished to install a wide-screen cinema complex

No longer voices in the wilderness — Friends of the Earth campaigners draw attention to the dangers of acid rain outside one of its major sources, a power station on Merseyside.

Ecological surveys, such as this at Cinderbarrow Tarn in Lancashire, broaden our understanding of how best to help preserve and restore our natural landscapes.

in the dome of St Paul's (or even sell chunks of the building as mementos for tourists), then was awarded hundreds of thousands of pounds a year for scrapping the plan and doing nothing. Yet that is the spirit of the system currently operating to 'protect' some of the UK's scarcest wildlife-rich places.

Direct action by government is also depleting the store still further. In terms of natural assets, it has been a case, not so much of selling off the family silver, but of using it as road bottoming. The victory for the integrity of London's oldest woodland over the march of the UK roads programme, at Oxleas Wood, was an unusual blip in an otherwise unrelenting onslaught on many wildlife havens elsewhere. The motorway gashes through Twyford Down, across Snelsmore Common and the ancient woods now severed by the Newbury Bypass, the five 'special' areas cut through by the M4 relief road on the Gwent Levels, and the 140 or so other choice wildlife places currently at risk from an expanding British roads network, suggest that, where wildlife interests are concerned, the ever-spiralling rise of the automobile is still, as the Wildlife Trusts have said, a matter of head-on collision.

Unfortunately, the rot doesn't stop simply at road level, appalling though the recent losses to tarmac may be. For as car ownership increases and journeys lengthen, vehicle transport is now the fastest growing source of carbon dioxide pollution in Britain and Ireland, and so is making an ever increasing contribution to global warming through the greenhouse effect.

About half the nitric oxide currently released into the UK air also comes from vehicles. This proportion is likely to rise as car numbers swell further, even as industry continues to improve its energy efficiency and reduces its emissions of pollutants. Transformed to nitrogen dioxide in the atmosphere, this pollution comes back to earth to acidify soils, mobilize potentially toxic aluminium and threaten the delicate balance of life in some of the dwindling band of locations with great richness of plant variety and scarce species.

Many places that are not under intensive agriculture and forestry, such as bogs, heaths and chalky or lime-rich grasslands, have relatively low supplies of nitrogen naturally available, and this plays a key role in maintaining the broad mix of plantlife there. Add extra nitrogen to such systems, and those plants which can thrive on it (such as nettles, goosegrass, red fescue and ryegrass) may quickly expand at the expense of less nitrogen-tolerant species. It is a poisoned chalice which kills variety. When kept topped-up by the atmospheric fallout of pollution from vehicles and other sources, even areas held sacrosanct as 'reserves' have no respite from it.

The same applies to other large-scale processes currently unfolding in the skies over Britain and Ireland as a direct result of pollution from human activities. Chemicals from refrigeration, air conditioning, dry cleaning and other sources have been eating away at the world's ozone layer for decades. Held in the stratosphere – some 3,000 metres above the level of Everest – this ozone absorbs much of the potentially harmful ultraviolet-B radiation in sunshine. When it thins, wild plants, crops, plankton and people could be at risk from these rays. In the early spring of 1996, ozone levels fell to the lowest concentration ever recorded over Britain. The consequences of continued thinning are uncertain, but deeply worrying.

More certain is the general progression of global warming, set in motion by greenhouse gases such as carbon dioxide. During the 1980s alone, the dubious accolade of warmest global year since records began was awarded five times. According to figures compiled by the United Nations Intergovernmental Panel which reviewed the scientific knowledge on this subject in the mid-1990s, even the most conservative estimates of global climate change forecast for the next century are faster than anything experienced in the last 10,000 years. The more pessimistic forecasts represent the speediest warming in 40 million years.

As oceans swell in the rising temperature and average sea levels rise, whole cultures on islands in the southern hemisphere could be obliterated. Big increases in forest fires, melting of ice caps and glaciers, poleward movement of climatic zones, and extinction of creatures and vegetation types not able to migrate or quickly adapt to changing conditions, are some other projected consequences now that the heat is on.

In Britain and Ireland, conditions are likely to be both warmer and wetter, both in summer and winter, by the middle of the next century, with the sea level perhaps one-third-of-a-metre (or about a foot) higher than at present. This shift will cause many changes, including pronounced alterations to both the lowest and the highest altitude wildlife refuges in these islands.

Coastal wetlands and saltmarshes, especially in south-east England, are already suffering from being squeezed between rising seas and unyielding shore defences. In the uplands, life forms that are intolerant of great cold and exposure are likely to advance uphill as air temperatures warm. As they do so, arctic-alpine flora and fauna could disappear. It is a sad irony that high altitude areas, at first glance the least affected by people, should be so peculiarly vulnerable to what could be the most widespread human-linked change yet set in motion on the planet.

Yet, despite the speed of predicted future fluctuations in climate, coping with change, holding it in check or going with its flow were, until very recently, of the very essence in human dealings with land and wildlife in Britain and Ireland. That is not to say that radical shifts in decades to come should be greeted with complacency, but rather that change, in itself, should not be seen as a total bogey. It could even be an opportunity, coaxing a radical rethink of our relationship with nature.

Many of the wildlife-rich areas described in this book have dwindled greatly through human action, both directly, through physical destruction, or indirectly, through pollution. But many of them also owed their former expansiveness to human action. People didn't instill the magic mix of life forms in them, but they surely helped special blends of wildlife

Opposite Left: A community nature park in King's Cross, central London.

Opposite Right: Conservation volunteers from Montgomeryshire Wildlife Trust restoring wetland at the Gaer in Powys.

to rise and spread and sparkle much more widely than would have been the case without human intervention.

In the natural course of ecological progression, and left unnibbled by domestic livestock or touched by the plough, many parts of Britain and Ireland, outwith the big blanket bogs, would be covered in trees and shrubs – not as a continuous canopy, but as a mosaic of forest and clearings, rivers and wetlands. When people stopped such succession in its tracks, turning it to their advantage for sources of animal fodder, meat, fuel and other raw materials, a host of places burgeoned. Downlands, meadows, reedbeds and fens, coppiced woods, lowland heaths and upland moors all thrived when there was a direct human involvement in their future.

Only in very recent generations have those close links been all but severed. The gulf between farmer and community, where producer and consumer are now so separated as to often find real difficulty in relating to each other, is one social consequence of this. But the severance has brought other widespread losses, both of the glorious medley of themes and variations which once testified to the natural diversity of British and Irish wildlife, and of the particular patterns of human association, both practical and cultural, which could in so many cases sustain it.

The qualities of a lowland heath in Hampshire, harbouring Dartford warblers and sand lizards and busy with warmth-loving insects, could not readily be translated to Scotland or western Ireland, for example. But the gradations of shading can be much subtler than that, as in the different blends of flowers in the meadows of different regions, counties, or (in the precious few areas where enough herb-infused greenswards remain) parishes.

Perhaps only in the range of tones and floral emphases in the extensive machair grasslands of the Hebrides can such transitions, coupled with intimate use by local townships, still be found on a large scale. They point to something very special indeed – that the natural communities of wildlife which thrive in response to certain patterns of human involvement can be as much an expression of the spirit of different places as can regional or local accents. Lose those wild communities and their association with people, and a primal *genius loci* goes too.

In that sense, it seems deeply appropriate that the most potent recent images of destruction of places like Twyford Down have come from the contact and conflict between groups of people so utterly different in appearance and behaviour as to defy neat categorization as the inhabitants of one country. When the Dongas Tribe met the 'security' forces on the ancient down, it symbolized, not just the battle for that particular place, important though that was, but a clash of world views – one revelling in the distinctiveness of different areas and cherishing links with the land, the other hell-bent on uniformity and ignoring those connections.

However strange the protagonists in such confrontations may seem, they focus attention on vitally important aspects of people's dealings with land and wildlife in Britain and Ireland at the close of the twentieth century. For it is now an inescapable fact that, at a time when many of the splendidly diverse communities of wildlife have been broken up and pushed to the brink of total annihilation, and when government-backed actions can add to that attrition, many people are working with renewed vigour and enthusiasm, both in groups and as individuals, to restore lost links with land and wildlife. State policies may be faltering, but the pace of local action seems firmer and more spirited than for decades.

Through that confident progress is coming, not simply a replay of former themes, performed in the precarious isolation of nature reserve stages, but the beginnings of a fundamental reshaping of the relationship between people, earth and diverse life forms. For what shrank to near vanishing point, especially in the last fifty years, is more than wildlife alone; more than distinctive and attractive places. It is the closeness of association between human communities and natural communities, between people's everyday life and the life of a wealth of different creatures. Those links are now being forged, affirmed, developed and celebrated again on a massive scale, giving a sense of energy and purpose to dealings with nature which is fundamentally different from the heavily science-based, and in some ways elitist, fixation with small and embattled 'special' sites of previous years.

That obsession was a product of particular times, and championing such rare and endangered places is still a necessary part of the overall thrust of nature conservation in Britain and Ireland. But it should now, quite clearly, not be the dominant part. For nature reserves, in some senses, are an admission of failure – a symbol that prime places for wildlife do not sit happily amongst the multifarious uses of the wider landscape. In times of rapid climatic change and government indifference to their fate, such reserves or designated wildlife areas have, at worst, become green ghettoes – precarious refuges for wildlife isolated from like communities elsewhere, and endangered by forces pressing-in from outside their boundaries. In conservation in the late 1990s, as in international politics, there is good reason to scorn the doublespeak of the 'safe haven'.

Rather, the many-faceted movement which is taking shape at this time is far more broadly based, and in its finest manifestations is both visionary and radical in outlook. The enthusiasm for expansion of native woodlands is one example of this, where huge schemes are already underway to create as well as restore, to expand as well as defend. When the forests of Cardiff, Leeds, Belfast and many other urban areas begin to burgeon within the next few years, millions of people will have easy access, some almost literally on their doorsteps, to woodlands and their associated wildlife.

The liberating influence of such new forests should not be underestimated, and in some ways is encapsulated in part of the stated aims of the Millennium Forest for Scotland scheme, which is acting as an umbrella for several hundred different projects, and aims to expand Scottish native woodlands by an awesome 100,000 hectares in the course of the next few years. Coupled with this growth, and with work on a further 50,000 hectares, the project will promote 'recreation, employment and training, artistic and cultural projects, research, education and innovative development of woodland products'.

That is no emergency schedule, drawn up to fend off assault on a fragmented resource,

Swansea Wildlife Action Group take part in 'A Walk for Wildlife' in West Glamorgan.

be made are not only of the direct kind, such as where human meets hedgehog on mutual home territory, but have wider potential to influence thought. They demonstrate that a restoration of qualities that so nearly were lost is not only possible, but is achievable in many different ways.

Whether on the railway embankments and cycle tracks which offer green lanes through urban spread, the native woodlands now sprouting where no timber has grown for centuries, the effluent lagoons where new reedbeds are flourishing, or the crofting townships and island estates where the land has been brought into community ownership for the first time in generations, people are acting in ways that benefit, rather than crush, land and wildlife.

The feelings of empowerment which are springing from a rediscovery of the vibrancy of the local and the varied, are sweet indeed when set against the losses of earlier years. For in times when many do not spend their whole lives in a single community, but move here and there as demands of work and other forces pull them, a sense of the distinctiveness of place can become more elusive and yet more urgently compelling.

Set adrift from generations of close contact with particular small areas, we can still warm to the things which mark one place as different from another; still yearn, as diaspora, for somewhere to take mental root. The wildlife and vegetation which gives surface expression to multifarious features of geology, soil, climate and history of human association within particular landscapes, both urban and rural, offers boundless potential for the rediscovery of a sense of community, both with wildlife and with ourselves.

Perhaps when such restoration has become widespread, and many current signs suggest that it will, then the time will come when an even greater leap of faith will be possible, somewhere in Britain and Ireland – that of allowing natural processes to take their own course, unfettered by the coaxing and cajoling of people, in a large tract of land. That would be strange territory indeed here, but one whose proclamation would signify a genuine easiness with life pulses far different from our own; an acceptance of another kind of natural heartland.

Such a state of place and mind still seems some way off. But in the here and now, I look again at my family's garden and the landscape which spreads beyond. It is a view I have known only briefly, and holds diverse wildlife and people with whom I have scarcely begun to form an acquaintance. But when my son points out a red fox crossing to the gorse in a neighbour's field and my daughter, still a toddler, smiles as she sees the wild geese in arrowed flight overhead, I know, in those moments, we've come home.

but a vigorous agenda for change, echoed and amplified in different ways by a characterful motley of other groups, such as Coed Cymru, Scottish Native Woods, Trees for Life and many more. Thanks also to the far-sighted ideas promoted by Common Ground – the body which, perhaps more than any other in Britain and Ireland, has brilliantly championed the glories of the locally distinctive through times of fixation with the rare and special – trees are again looming large as important elements in the cultural life and seasonal round of events in many places.

Through such work to bring trees and people back together, both physically and culturally, a great deal of wildlife will benefit, for woodlands can provide ideal routeways for creatures to move in and across areas that were once unwelcoming to them. In the days of the information superhighway and the digital domains of the Internet, it is amusing to think that natural networks – of leaf and branch, stem and water – are now prominent in the thinking of many who are concerned to restore connections for and with wildlife.

Such networks could literally be life-savers for scarce creatures as the climate changes, giving escape routes from the old green ghettoes. But their potential for life enhancement goes much further. As such corridors are restored, created, expanded and joined-up, scope for contact with wildlife of many kinds grows and changes. And the connections that can

A nesting mute swan in a community wetland at Abergele in North Wales.